RADICAL
SENDING

RADICAL SENDING

Go to Love and Serve

DEMI PRENTISS and FLETCHER LOWE

Morehouse Publishing
NEW YORK

Morehouse Publishing, 19 East 34th Street, New York, NY 10016
Morehouse Publishing is an imprint of Church Publishing Incorporated.
www.churchpublishing.org

Cover design by Laurie Klein Westhafer
Interior design and typesetting by Beth Oberholtzer

Library of Congress Cataloging-in-Publication Data
A catalog record of this book is available from the Library of Congress.
ISBN-13: 978-0-8192-3184-0 (pbk.)
ISBN-13: 978-0-8192-3185-7 (ebook)

Printed in the United States of America

*With grateful hearts, we dedicate this book
to our amazing spouses, Mary Fran and Paul*

*To our intrepid colleagues in Episcopalians
on Baptismal Mission: Peyton Craighill,
Herbert Donovan, Edward Lee,
Wayne Schwab, and Craig Smith*

*To those "radical sending" congregations — past, present,
and yet-to-come — who equip the saints for ministry*

*And to those saints who bear good fruit
in every aspect of their daily lives.*

Contents

Appendices

Foreword

The summer of 2003 marked a watershed moment for The Episcopal Church. With the election of V. Gene Robinson as bishop of New Hampshire—the first openly gay, partnered bishop in the Anglican Communion—we flung the doors wider and declared ourselves a church for others: gay and lesbian people, but also many others who had felt rejected, alienated, or wondered just how big God's embrace could get.

The same summer, I began the research that led to the publication of *Radical Welcome*.

As I write these words, The Episcopal Church is marking the weeks until the 2015 General Convention. I am struck by how far we have come in these twelve years, how mainstream it has become in many quarters to speak of embracing The Other, cultivating humility, releasing privilege, and allowing our churches to be transformed by authentic relationship with the changing local contexts where we dwell.

But the Spirit isn't finished with us. Just as we begin to imagine how gifts from emerging generations and cultures could shift Episcopal worship, leadership, ministries, and identity, just as we swing the doors open to embrace new communities within, we also have to reimagine walking out those same open doors into our daily lives. In other words, radical welcome is incomplete if it's not paired with radical sending.

Demi Prentiss and Fletcher Lowe are the ideal pair to guide congregations deeper into this commitment. Both have spent decades fiercely dedicated to celebrating the ministry of the laity as the primary Christian ministry. They understand that we worship God, serve God, embody God, and meet God in our daily lives. Does this diminish what happens inside our congregations? Absolutely not. It simply makes real what our theology proclaims: The prayers and sacramental acts that happen inside church are a rehearsal for the way we live as Christ's body beyond the church. Or, as they put it, "When the words and actions [of worship] are truly life giving, their power cannot be contained inside the building. When the liturgy comes to life, the liturgy becomes connected to life." Christians should exit those church doors ready to serve as living signs of God's grace and to see all of life as sacred.

In *Radical Sending*, Demi and Fletcher offer an array of practices, reflections, stories, and resources for individuals and congregations that seek to understand Christian vocation afresh. Church was never supposed to be just what we do inside a building or at a particular time on a Sunday. Church is who we are every moment, in every place.

What makes this sending so radical? To begin, it reverses the colonial impulse to walk about like Lady Bountiful, the benefactor with gifts and wisdom that she graciously hands to the underprivileged masses. Instead, Demi and Fletcher bring the wisdom of community organizing and the Faith at Work movement to the forefront. They reveal pathways for walking alongside our neighbors, listening for their gifts, asking questions with genuine curiosity about the other, seeking God's will in Scripture, practicing with our own gifts, and sometimes even holding back in order to welcome others to practice their gifts.

But it's not just the "how" that makes this sending so radical. It's also the "who" and the "where." Every Christian is sent, by virtue of our baptism. In this reimagined paradigm, there are no second-class citizens, and certainly there are no second-class Christians. How much have we limited God's power working in us by reserving the title of "minister" for the 0.8 percent who are ordained? Demi and Fletcher hear God's call to unleash the 99.2 percent who make up the laity, sending teams of world-changing disciples trekking forth to join up with God's mission in Christ.

And if you think that mission is reserved for outreach ministries or explicitly churchy activities, think again. God is claiming and healing the whole creation, and that means God is already moving in our neighborhoods, families, workplaces, commercial enterprises, civic and recreational spaces, and community gatherings. *Radical Sending* recounts story after story of ordinary radical people of faith who take God's call seriously enough to carry it into every part of their lives.

Perhaps the word "radical" will sound a bit off-putting or even "hard-edged" to the ears of good church folk. That may be so, but we're called, equipped, and sent in the name of Jesus Christ, the original radical. Thanks to Demi and Fletcher's visionary work here, Christ's radical calling should feel just a little more possible. May all those who read this book feel deeply, beautifully, radically welcomed *and* sent to love and serve God. Alleluia and amen!

The Reverend Canon Stephanie Spellers

† Introduction to Radical Sending

Our Journey to Radical Sending

Stephanie Spellers's 2006 book *Radical Welcome* has provided a much-needed guide and goad to congregations to look beyond their "friendly" label to analyze the true quality of their welcome. Inspired by the lessons of that book, many congregations have reframed their understanding of what "being church" means, especially in extending radical hospitality to those who might be understood as "other."

As a "bookend" to *Radical Welcome*'s groundbreaking message, we have chosen to examine how congregations might reclaim their role in sending the people of God into the world. Congregations whose hearts have been opened to offer radical welcome to all God's people are uniquely qualified to send those very people out, proclaiming God's Good News. To preach the message of "radical sending." As the Presbyterian minister proclaimed, dismissing his Sunday flock, "The worship is over, the service begins."

But first, we offer a little background about our own journeys.

Demi's Story

In mid-2000, the large downtown Episcopal congregation where I was serving discerned a call to be the church not only for our members, but also for the neighborhood. The church's location was a busy area of downtown San Antonio, Texas, surrounded by office buildings and hotels, the city convention center, and a major communications infra-structure hub. Some congregations might have chosen to focus on the homeless population that gathered just outside our doors, who were

3

served by a coalition of churches including our own. A much larger group of people spent a large chunk of their lives just beyond our walls from 8:00 a.m. to 5:00 p.m., Monday through Friday. From our vantage point, it seemed that no one in the faith community was paying much attention to these workers. The church leadership chose to focus energy and resources on how people engaged in their daily work might become intentional Christians in their workplace—whether that was an office, a factory, a home, a hospital, or a construction site. That focus gave birth to the Center for Faith in the Workplace, which over time spun off as The Work+Shop, a separate nonprofit ministry.

My role in helping midwife that ministry brought me into contact with people like John Lewis, Paul Minus, and Pete Hammond, core players in the Coalition for Ministry in Daily Life (CMDL). In the late 1990s and 2000s, the CMDL promoted, as its mission statement affirmed, "that all Christians have been called into ministry and that for most of them their arena of ministry is in and to the world."[1] Its members were drawn from organizations, campus ministries, seminaries and colleges, and individuals from a range of Christian traditions, largely in the USA. Those creative souls—many clergy, some laity— were working on the margins of the church, building bridges between the church as institution and a world that was growing increasingly suspicious of all things churchy. While the mainline churches were becoming increasingly fearful of impending irrelevance, advances in telecommunications and the expanding reach of the Internet were redefining community and bringing the world inside our living rooms.

As a lay professional working in the church, I found all of this foment enormously exciting and hope-inspiring. The voices that were preaching and teaching daily life ministry affirmed my understanding of humanity—that we were created as the image and likeness of God in order to do God's work in every aspect of our lives. I had grown up attending a large Episcopal church in Houston, Texas. I had somehow received the message that my confirmation conveyed an obligation to be active in ministry. My tribe of Episcopalians was "high" enough to fully believe that Christ was truly present in the bread and wine of communion. But we were "low" enough to see little distinction between the priest and the laity. We were all meant to work at making Christ truly present in the work we did and the places where we lived and moved and had our being—to "become what we had received" (though we never would have expressed the thought in those words).

My father—a lawyer in love with the law, who thought the Magna Carta was the greatest document created by the mind of man—understood his vocation to be a calling worthy of a Christian. Because of that, my working with the Ministry in Daily Life folks was, in some senses, like "coming home" to an understanding of "call" that wasn't restricted to those who were seeking ordination.

One of the "edge-walkers" I met during that time was author and publisher Greg Pierce, whose book *The Mass Is Never Ended*[2] helped transform my understanding of liturgy. He points to the Dismissal at the end of the Mass ("Go in peace to love and serve the Lord.") as the essential moment in the liturgy, the culmination of all that has gone before. Those words are to send us "like a cannonball" into the world and our daily lives, having been prayed for, taught, forgiven, healed, and fed, to embrace our daily mission of transforming and reconciling in Christ's name.

At the same time as I was reclaiming my childhood understanding of Christian vocation, I was earning a degree in congregational development from Seabury-Western Seminary. My passion for congregational development had drawn me to enroll in the DMin program. My history of ministry development and community organizer training had led Arlin Rothauge, then-director of the Institute for Congregational Development, to okay my admission despite my not holding an MDiv degree. My class, the third in the Institute's history, included two laity and thirty clergy, and all of us brought at least ten years' experience in congregational ministry. Only four of us were women.

For the congregational development DMin, we gathered for three weeks each summer, three years running, immersing ourselves in twelve-hour days of classes, small group sessions, and meals with our instructors that turned into seminars. Sometime during the second session of the three summer residential intensives, we learned that because of accreditation issues, laypeople who didn't hold an MDiv degree would no longer be admitted to the program. My small group compadres—three rectors—were aghast. My degree process wasn't threatened and the decision had no impact on my continuing in the program. Still, they took the news personally, on my behalf. "We've learned so much from her," they said, affirming not only my theological opinions (which they didn't always share) but also my viewpoint as one of the 99.2 percent—those in the church who are not ordained.[3] They claimed that the program as a whole would suffer without lay participants, and I took that as a high compliment as well as affirmation that ordination wasn't required in order to "do theology."

My seminary education helped codify for me the bedrock of my theology—my belief in the Incarnation and in God's economy. God's self-emptying act of becoming fully human—the Incarnation—absolutely affirms, for me, the goodness of the world that God created and is still creating. And Jesus's humanity has, for all time, sanctified human activity in service of God's mission. We, as precious children of God, are invited to participate in the life-giving dance of the Trinity, as we acknowledge and incarnate God's life-giving activity in every part of our lives.

God's economy working in the world means that absolutely nothing is lost. No tear, no suffering, no celebration, no effort is meaningless in God's eternity-based household. "We know that in all things God works for good" (Rom. 8:28a NIV). God operates just as thoroughly, just as transformationally, through our workaday lives as in our church-based actions. "Bidden or unbidden, God is present," to quote Erasmus.

All of these threads come together, for me, in what some call the "ministry in daily life movement." Those CMDL pioneers expressed it as connecting Sunday to Monday—embodying our Christianity in our everyday lives, so that those around us see our faith in action. Not so much as heroic, "ministry-to" work that allows us to cast ourselves in the role of Lady Bountiful, but more as day-by-day, "ministry-with" partnerships that call on us to walk alongside, and learn from, those among whom we practice ministry. As a facilitator of Christian formation, I am concerned that often we settle for teaching people tenets of the faith without calling forth the transformation that occurs when we take on the hard work of actually being Jesus-followers—people who practice faithful patterns of life, modeled by Jesus. Those practices are truly life-giving: listening, opening space for, asking curious questions, speaking from our own experience, inviting, forbearing, looking deeply into Scripture. And perhaps even stepping away from practicing our own gifts, in order to let someone else do that ministry.

That's where "radical sending" comes in. Communities that intentionally work at such life-giving practices among themselves prepare their members to be the salt and leaven and light sent forth into the everyday world. Such communities are focused on making disciples—genuine followers of The Way of Jesus—so that they might be sent out as apostles—those who are sent out.

This book emerges out of my ambition for the Church—the body of Christ—to learn to be such a community. I long to see communities where living as just such a body is their reason for being. I hope you'll join me in the work of discovering, forming, and sustaining such expressions of the body of Christ.

Fletcher's Story

Upon graduating from seminary, I was assigned by my bishop to be the vicar of a small congregation in Seneca, Oconee County, South Carolina, near Clemson University—best noted for being the home of the 22nd presiding bishop of the Episcopal Church, John E. Hines (1965–74). It was a congregation of caring folks who nurtured, supported, and endured me as both newly ordained and newly married.

During my formative four-and-a-half years there, some seventeen northern industries relocated to that sleepy southern county, which had a transforming urbanizing effect on its rural life. As a congregation we began creatively to live into that new reality captured in *The Episcopalian's* November 1963 cover story, "Seneca's Rurban Revolution." Many of the managers for the relocating companies arrived ahead of their families. I found that the best way to connect with them was in their offices, hence I began workplace visits that developed into conversations connecting their faith with their work. A Seneca banker put it this way, "I try to test my decisions by thinking what Christ would do in my place here. The vicar has tried to teach us to look at our jobs in that way and I think it works." A factory manager reflected, "If you really try to be a Christian in your work, it makes it a lot harder—but I wouldn't have it any other way."

That experience set the tone for my ongoing pastoral, liturgical, and educational ministry in the other congregations I have served as we raised up the vocation and calling of all the baptized in their daily lives. For example, liturgically, we reclaimed the Sixth Sunday of Easter as Rogation Sunday, drawing on its earlier traditions of celebrating the means of production in the farming and fishing communities by celebrating the means of production in the textile and banking and media businesses. On those Sundays, all were invited to place a small token of their ministry in an alms basin that was blessed. We also designed a liturgy and a litany celebrating, blessing, and affirming those for their ministries. Along the way, I have been called to use a house blessing format to "bless" places like a newspaper office, a paving company's facilities, and an architect's office building.

In John's Prologue, he writes: "And the Word became flesh and lived among us," or as the Greek puts it: "and pitched his tent among us." The Incarnate Lord, Emmanuel, God with us is in each and every aspect of our lives. Thus the sacraments in the Episcopal tradition are not just two major and five minor, but infinite in their possibilities, for all of life is sacramental—outward and visible signs of inward and spiritual grace—including life on the job, in the home, in the community, and in the church. So Paul calls on the Christian community in Ephesus to "equip the saints for the work of ministry" (Eph. 4:12).

The more my ministry became focused on affirming this ministry of saints, I began to seek out others who shared this vision. That led me to Bill Diehl's first book, *Thank God, It's Monday* (Minneapolis: Fortress Press, 1982), which tells of how he gained great affirmation for his leadership roles within the Lutheran church, locally and nationally, but never was his life as a steel industry executive affirmed or recognized. Through Bill, I became an early participant in the formation of the Coalition for Ministry in Daily Life (CMDL) that Demi has mentioned. Its annual conferences were true watering holes for me as I met, talked with, and gained affirmation and ideas from others committed to the ministry of daily life. They also were reality checks—that much of the church did not "get it," and that a good deal of my excitement for this sense of ministry was not shared to a large extent by the church regardless of denomination, including the Episcopal Church.

At the 2005 meeting of the CMDL, several of us Episcopalians discussed the possibility of meeting a day before the 2006 meeting to explore organizing an Episcopal component of the Coalition. That happened and *Episcopal Partners for Faithfulness in Daily Life* was initiated, led by a small steering committee. Its purposes were/are:

1. To provide a communications link between partners to share programs, ideas, concerns, needs, and more.

2. To be a prophetic voice and a resource for furthering faithfulness in daily life within the Episcopal Church.

Demi and I were on its initial steering committee and have continued to serve as the organization has evolved, now renamed *Episcopalians on Baptismal Mission*. The steering committee continues to meet every five to six weeks via conference call, despite the end of the CMDL in 2011.

Over the years in congregations I have served, several pastoral, educational, liturgical, and communication efforts were made to affirm and support the ministries of all the baptized. Some of those congregation-tested ideas were included in the Episcopal Church's publication *Ministry in Daily Life; A Guide to Living the Baptismal Covenant* (New York: Domestic and Foreign Missionary Society, 1996) that I coedited with Linda Grenz. Ten years later I published *Baptism: The Event and the Adventure, from the Font into Daily Life* (Leeds, MA: LeaderResources, 2006) as an e-book.

In 2014, the congregation in Richmond, Virginia, where I have served as a priest-in-residence had as its theme *Radical Welcome* using Stephanie Spellers's book of the same name (New York: Church Publishing, 2006) as a guide to help members focus on "come." As I walked along with the congregation in its work to develop more welcoming practices, I began to sense that there needed to be a complementary book that focused on "go," hence this book on radical sending of the baptized into their daily lives "to do the work God has given us to do" (Book of Common Prayer [hereafter BCP], 366).

Join the Journey

We invite you to come along as we explore the theological foundations for understanding the church as "radically sent," as well as the implications for the church's life in community. Although there may be references to the Episcopal Church's liturgy, they are simply illustrative of the vision that can be found within every Christian denomination. Part I lays the theological framework—tapping Scripture, reason, and tradition—for this vision of the church. The work of emergent /emerging churches and the missional church movement is finding expression in communities of faith which are not only called together but also sent out into the communities where they are rooted.

Part II offers a range of examples where radical sending is practiced—in the traditions of Celtic Christians, Lutherans, Mennonites, and Roman Catholics; in congregations; and in the lives of individuals who understand themselves as "sent." In addition, we'll take a look at some of the limiting assumptions of church institutions that can pose obstacles to faith communities developing a culture of radical sending.

Part III proposes strategies and tactics for moving toward building faith communities that equip their members to be salt and light wherever they find themselves. Chapters deal with recognizing the unspoken curriculum that our churches follow, discovering strategies for offering a new vision, dealing with the inevitable difficulties, and celebrating the vastly expanded horizon for faith.

We encourage you to join us on this journey. At the end of each chapter you will find questions in a section titled "Going Forth." You're invited to use these as starters for your own reflection, for group discussion, or as a framework for a class or retreat built around this book. Perhaps you'll take the opportunity to blog or journal about them. Each group of questions begins with noticing, then moves to analysis, reflection, discussion or discernment, and an opportunity for action.

May this resource serve to fuel your engagement with the challenge of adding the word "sending" to the definition of how to be a life-giving Christian community and inspire your imaginative response. Visit www.RadicalSending.com to access our resources and offer your stories to the growing "radical sending" community.

The Church's Journey to Radical Sending

Radical Sending. *Sending*: it is the propelling forth of the baptized to live into their faith in their daily lives. As Jesus instructed, "As you (Father) have sent me into the world, so have I sent them into the world" (John 17:18). *Radical*: it is radical because it calls on a congregation to be intentional about its pastoral, liturgical, and formation life in light of the Dismissal in the Episcopal Eucharistic liturgy: "send us out" and "let us go forth" (BCP, 366). By that we do *not* mean a congregation's outreach or mission efforts. That is for another book. Rather, we are calling for congregations to "equip the saints for ministry" (Eph. 4:12) in their own daily lives of work and leisure and community and school and family. That may call on a congregation to make a paradigm shift in its communal life. Our hope is that we will provide some ways and means both to support those congregations that "get it" in terms of becoming a sending congregation and to provide resources for those that want to "get it."

So how did we get to where we are and why may there be something radical about getting where we want to be? Before we explore these questions, let us take a moment for a short biblical word study. Throughout the New Testament all the baptized are referred to as the *laos*, the people of God. A close New Testament synonym was *kleros*, "used to describe the dignity and appointment of all the people to ministry."[4] There may have been functions within the *laos* (presider, deacon, bishop), but all were within the *laos*, the *kleros*. Later, as functions began to become more institutionalized, the word *kleros* evolved into the way of separating the ordained from the nonordained.[5]

11

In at least one diocesan prayer cycle people are asked to pray for "the congregation and clergy of . . ." almost as though the clergy are not to be considered part of the congregation. With that in mind, let us now look in on some of the church's history. To do so, we must begin with baptism.

The Early Church

The norm in the early church was adult baptism. In the Acts of the Apostles adults came to be baptized affirming their belief in Jesus as Lord, the result of the teaching and preaching of witnesses to the risen Christ. The post–New Testament journey for adults toward their baptism was known as the *catechumenate*, a word meaning "listening with the ear." The catechumens went through an extensive period (often three years) of reflection, discernment, and instruction focused on the life and death and resurrection of Jesus, the Messiah. That preparation was centered in their (1) renunciation of the existing cultural worldview and its values, (2) exploration of the Christian worldview and the values of the kingdom of God, and (3) taking on that kingdom view by being incorporated into the body of Christ, the Church, through baptism. They became a part of the *laos*, the *kleros*, the people of God. The impact of their new life in Christ inevitably necessitated change and, for some, meant finding a new vocation and breaking off certain relationships, even those of their blood family. Not only was a Christian "marked as Christ's own forever," but also because of that baptismal commitment, the newly baptized person was often marked by the existing culture as an outsider, subject to isolation, persecution, and perhaps even death. To "put on Christ" was to risk one's life—literally to deny oneself, take up one's cross, and follow Christ into uncharted waters. It was not an easy journey, this early church paradigm, but each pilgrim emerged with a deep sense of how being a Christian directly affected every aspect of daily life.

Constantinian Christianity

With Constantine (274–337 CE) as emperor of the Roman Empire, the paradigm began to change. The good news was that the persecution of Christians came to an end. The other news was mixed: The realm, by the edict of Milan (313), became "Christian." The focus on baptism shifted from the extensive catechumenal paradigm of the individual candidate to more instantaneous mass baptisms, often of entire tribes, even nations, by the decree of a local ruler, sometimes under the threat of the sword.

As baptism became an expected social norm with little preparation or nurture, the call to be a "real Christian" began to shift to those who took on special vows for the ordained or the monastic life. The term *kleros* (clergy) came to be used to distinguish those who were separated from the rest of the *laos* (laity) by their greater commitment. As Thomas Ray, retired bishop of Northern Michigan, has pointed out, "For the first four centuries, the catechumenate was the structure through which people came into baptism. Since then, we have flip-flopped that over to holy orders where the same conditions exist: long preparation times (three years of seminary education or its equivalent), new names (the Reverend), new garments (the stole), new vocations. The old catechumenate has been replaced by ordination!"[6] Thus, the focus on the minor sacrament of holy orders supplanted the major sacrament of baptism as the expression of true Christian commitment, demoting baptism and elevating ordination.

The practical effects of this Constantinian paradigm have resulted in some far-reaching practical shifts in the life of the Church, which continue to this day. "Holy orders" came to represent where the real action in the Christian community centered, dominated by the *kleros* (deacons, priests, and bishops), while the role for the *laos* (laity) was understood as being supportive of the "ministry" of the clergy. There are sixteen centuries of church history filled with illustrations of this paradigm of prerogatives and privileges afforded the clergy. For example, The Episcopal Church's triennial General Convention, its most important legislative body, is three-fourths clergy: the House of Bishops (all clergy) and the House of Deputies (half clergy). Most Episcopal diocesan conventions are likewise clergy dominated—all diocesan clergy are typically participants amidst a small specially elected group of the nonordained. Yet clergy represent only 0.8 percent of Episcopalians.[7] A look at other denominations reflected a similar clergy-dominated structure. The Episcopal services of ordination, especially those for bishops, are far more elaborate and require considerably more planning and coordination than anything comparable for baptism.

The medium is the message. And irony of ironies, there is nothing in the entire service of ordination for bishop, priest, or deacon in the 1979 Book of Common Prayer that even remotely acknowledges that the one seeking ordination has been baptized (although this is stipulated in The Episcopal Church's canons). It is easy to see how far we have disconnected ordination from its baptismal roots. The clergy, to borrow from Paul's analogy of the body of Christ, have become disproportionately enlarged members of the body, be it ear or nose or leg or arm, while the rest of the body—the nonordained—are shriveled: a gross distortion. The Constantinian paradigm is alive and well today.

What then about the nonordained, the laity, under this Constantinian paradigm? As the sacrament of "Holy Orders" has superseded baptism as *the* sacrament defining the "true believers," the role of the nonordained has become increasingly devalued. "Lay ministry" has often evolved into what laypeople can do to help the clergy do their job in perpetuating the life of the congregation as an institution. Terms like "mutual ministry" and "shared leadership" more often than not apply to the local church as the place where all ministry takes place. Rarely do laypersons see what they do in the world as ministry. After all, ministry is what clergy do; they are the real ministers; they provide the ministry while the laity receive. And so, in describing themselves the nonordained have been known to say, "I am *just* a layperson!" Thus, "the whole sense of ministry has been collapsed upon the ordained," Bishop Ray concludes.[8]

Emerging Christianity

Where in our world today do we go to recover and rediscover the ministry of all the baptized? We need a new paradigm.

The experience of the early Christian community can teach us. In that paradigm, it was through their baptism that those early Christians literally changed worlds, changed direction, changed focus. Conversion was a transformation to a new worldview marked by the sign of the cross. As the baptized of today, that is our calling too. As the community of the baptized, we find our identity in being "marked as Christ's own forever" (BCP, 308).

The decades-long decline of the Church in Europe can also teach us. Following the Enlightenment and the Industrial Revolution, the Church, with some notable exceptions, has come to be perceived as irrelevant in the daily lives of the people. As the middle-class population increased and daily work moved beyond the home and the farm, the Church has found itself on the margins of the culture.

There is a *relevant* lesson in that for us. For example, when we meet someone new, our first question often is, "What is your name?" The conversation then usually moves to, "What do you do?" Congregations have been good at asking the first—we get names on pew cards, we send visiting teams to newcomers, we write letters of welcome. But when do we take that second question seriously? Not often enough. In years of visiting parishioners in their workplaces, I (Fletcher) lead with, "What do you do here?" That is followed by, "What is the connection between what you do here and your faith—the Sunday-Monday connection?" In my experience, for nearly 85 percent of individuals asked, that is the first time the connection question has been raised. Why is it that the Church has generally failed to connect with where the baptized spend most of their God-given time and talent? No wonder the Church is perceived as irrelevant. It is that Sunday-to-Monday disconnect that calls for a new paradigm.

If, in fact, baptism is *the* sacramental act that declares, "you are . . . marked as Christ's own forever" (BCP, 308), then the process of living into that identity becomes *the* primary responsibility of the Christian community. As Theodore Eastman, retired bishop of the Diocese of Maryland, has written, "The sacrament of Baptism is the ordination of the Christian to ministry. . . . It is the process of ignition that propels each Christian into the world in his or her own way and time."[9]

It is time for the Church to do some radical rethinking! What about this: Within the Episcopal Church's baptismal liturgy comes a question for the community: "Will you who witness these vows do all in your power to support these persons in their life in Christ?" What would a congregation look like if it saw as its job description "supporting of the baptized in their daily life in Christ?"

And what if a congregation understood as its mission statement, "We take the Dismissal seriously," as a way of living into the closing words of the Episcopal Church's Eucharistic liturgy: "send us out" and "let us go forth."

Any congregation that chose to do so would be challenging the Church's prevailing Constantinian paradigm, with its hierarchical relationship between nonordained and ordained. This would necessitate a radical redefinition of that relationship. Such redefinition calls for the *kleros* once again to be seen as part of the *laos*, with its specific calling to "equip the saints for the work of ministry." That would mean a reordering of the pastor's priorities, taking on the role of outward-focused servant ministry, serving the members of the congregation in their ministries in the world. The pastor would then become the assistant to the people for their ministries. "Ministry," "calling," "vocation" would become terms applicable to all the *laos*, not just the ordained. After all, it is God's ministry to which all the baptized are called, called to share as God's people (*laos*). In such a reality, there are no second-class Christians. Under this post-Constantinian paradigm, the work of the congregation, under the leadership of the servant pastor, is to nurture and equip and empower the baptized for their ministry in their worlds of home, community, leisure, work, and school.

To again quote Bishop Ray, "We are a 'chosen race, a royal priesthood, a holy nation, God's own people,' that we may declare the wonderful deeds of him who has called us out of darkness into his marvelous light. And he calls us friends, brothers and sisters, to share his reconciled, serving, apostolic love, 'for better or for worse, for richer, for poorer, in sickness and in health,' for life, and for life everlasting!"[10]

Therefore, to paraphrase the words of sending that conclude worship, "Let us go forth into *our worlds of daily life*, rejoicing in the power of the Spirit. Thanks be to God!!"

✝

PART I

The Theology of
Radical
Sending

The Base Camp

God is calling us to strengthen the ministries of
our congregations . . . as the spiritual base camps
where we gather for inspiration and renewal
and strength, and from which we go out to
help Christ heal and reconcile the world.

THE RIGHT REVEREND MARIANN EDGAR BUDDE,
SERMON TO THE EPISCOPAL DIOCESE OF WASHINGTON,
NOVEMBER 13, 2011

Hikers who do serious mountain climbing, like scaling Denali in
Alaska or the Himalayas in Nepal, know how important a base
camp is, how dependent they are on what it provides for their journey. Even nonhikers can imagine a list of what they find helpful and
supportive:

- A staging area, launch pad, resting place, respite for
  restoring the spirit
- A safe haven, refuge from the storm, warmth, hospitality
- Encouragement, affirmation, celebration
- A nurturing environment for coming, going, returning
- Regrouping, retooling, restoring, refueling, renewing,
  rejuvenation
- Provisions: equipment, tools, repairs, food, and other supplies
- Training and acclimatization
- Healing when injured, emergency care

- Maps, guidance as to what is ahead
- Communications center, a place to share stories, connection with other base camps
- Community, fellowship

Impressive: A base camp can mean the difference between making an ascent and having to give up, between celebration and failure, between life and death.

Now take another look at that list. What would you strike as not being applicable for a congregation? The vast majority of this list reflects what any faith community would like to see as its reason for being.

From a Christian perspective, then, let us look at the base camp as a metaphor for the local congregation. Presbyterian pastor Steve Jacobsen put it this way:

> One image that may be useful is that of the church as a base camp. . . . The church is a base camp in which a community of people gathers to reflect on life, be reminded of their identity, and make plans for exploration. From there, each person goes out during the week to take on that part of the mountain that is theirs to explore. The base camp exists to *serve* the climbing team. In itself, it is neither the goal of the expedition nor the mountain itself. The value of this image is that it affirms the importance of the community . . . but does not mistake the institution for the central reality. The hikers don't exist for the good of the base camp. The base camp exists for the good of the hikers. The implications of this view of the church's role for working people are clear. The church needs to focus on its timeless tasks: it is to be a place of worship, education and community. But it also needs to evaluate how well it is empowering people for the work on the mountain those other six days. The church exists for the people, not the reverse. People deserve our help in making sense of all seven days."[11]

Let's be clear about what Jacobsen is saying, and what the base camp metaphor (as congregation) teaches us: The hikers (members) don't exist for the good of the base camp (faith community). The base camp exists for the good of the hikers.

We in the church often get that reversed. We may be good at paying lip service to lay ministry in daily life, but our actions speak louder than our words. We act as though the role of hiker/layperson is to help the pastor succeed in running the base camp. What if, instead, the ideal was for the pastor to support hikers/laypersons in living into their baptism in all the aspects of daily life? The concept of the congregation as base camp then calls on the ordained to move beyond concerns for a congregation's survival and programming, to see their role as "equipping the saints for the work of ministry" (Eph. 4:12) in their day-to-day hiking/baptismal journeys. The Christian life is not unlike the hiker's journey with its straight and crooked places, its peaks and valleys, its potholes and smooth places. And every hiker needs the support of a base camp in order to engage in the journey.

When we understand the congregation as a base camp, the focus of the congregation's life shifts away from making sure the congregation survives and thrives. Its priority becomes the support of the hikers on their life's journeys. The congregation is not therefore the destination, but a way station, staging area, watering hole, launch pad for the journey. The base camp (congregation) is a safe place and shelter—a place of refuge, renewal, regrouping, recommitment, restoring, refueling, retooling, refreshment, re-creation, and respite for reviving the spirit. It is a place of healing, emergency care, and repair; it is integral to the hikers' world, providing a bridge from liturgy to life. The base camp exists for the hikers. Their journeys are taken seriously. Worship becomes sustenance for the hard work of the climb. The Word is food for the spirit. The Bread and Wine are food for the journey.

The hike is wherever the baptized person spends time living life— work, family, community, school, leisure, and wider world. That is why the hike matters to God. Those are the venues where hikers spends their God-given gifts of time, talent, and ability. As in the Eucharist, Christ is really present in those places. "The Word became flesh and dwelt among us." It is the base camp's (congregation's) mission to guide, support, and equip the hiker to live into that presence.

As with all metaphors, so with the base camp: It has its limitations. Unlike the Denali base camps, those working in the congregational base camp include not only those hired, but also many of the "hikers" who volunteer for liturgical, formation, and pastoral care ministries. But the focus of the metaphor is not lost. The vision is still on how those "in house" ministries are equipping the hikers for their callings in their daily lives.

The Lord is my *Sherpa;* I shall not want.

The Hiker's Commissioning

One expression of the hiker's commissioning is embedded in the Episcopal Church's catechism (BCP, 855).

> Q. Who are the ministers of the Church?
> A. The ministers of the Church are lay persons, bishops, priests, and deacons.
> Q. What is the ministry of the laity?
> A. The ministry of lay persons is to represent Christ and his Church; to bear witness to him wherever they may be; and, according to the gifts given them, to carry on Christ's work of reconciliation in the world; and to take their place in the life, worship, and governance of the Church.

The Book of Common Prayer lists laypersons as the first mentioned ministers: before bishops, before priests, before deacons. Notice too that the priorities of their ministry are "worldly," and that the "churchy" functions are left for last: "to take their place in the life, worship, and governance of the Church." Preceding that are the crucial ways that the laity live out their faith in the world—their hikes: "To represent Christ and his Church; to bear witness to him wherever they may be; and, according to the gifts given them, to carry on Christ's work of reconciliation in the world." The very insightful layperson Verna Dozier put it this way:

> Laypeople carry out those functions in the church (e.g., assist in the liturgy, serve on the vestry, teach church school, etc.), but to me they are always secondary functions for laity. The layperson's primary function is out there in the world.[12]

Jean Haldane, another layperson, reflected, "Let us see the laity as people who must be nurtured for ministry in society rather than as recruits for tasks in and for the church."[13] The key question then for a congregation, the Christian's base camp, is how it is preparing, equipping, enhancing, affirming, and supporting its laity, its hikers, in their journey, in their primary ministry in the world to which they have been commissioned by their baptism—work, leisure, family, school, community, and wider world. It is for this ministerial/missional priority in the world that the base camp exists. For some this may call for a paradigm shift.

The Hiker's Job Description

The Book of Common Prayer uses the Baptismal Covenant (pp. 304–5) as its primary job description for hikers with parallels in other denominations, such as the Evangelical Lutheran Church in America's *Evangelical Lutheran Worship* (pp. 232–44). The orientation of the Covenant is significant. First comes the Baptismal (Apostles') Creed. This foundational declaration roots each baptized person in an historic statement of faith. This sets the tone for why we, as Christians, live as we do. We are not humanists or atheists, promising to act for the greater good of society. We are first and foremost Christians, living out our lives rooted and grounded in the context of our faith in the Triune God: Father, Son, and Holy Spirit. It is that faith, which undergirds all that comes after, the *raison d'être*, the motivation for all that follows in the Covenant. We carry out the rest because of our belief *in* God: Father, Son, Holy Spirit. In the context of the Episcopal liturgy the entire congregation, in making this ancient baptismal statement of faith, joins the person being baptized, supported and accompanied by sponsors.

Celebrant Do you believe in God the Father?
People I believe in God, the Father almighty,
creator of heaven and earth.
Celebrant Do you believe in Jesus Christ, the Son of God?
People I believe in Jesus Christ, his only Son, our Lord.
He was conceived by the power of the Holy Spirit
and born of the Virgin Mary.
He suffered under Pontius Pilate,
was crucified, died, and was buried.
He descended to the dead.
On the third day he rose again.
He ascended into heaven,
and is seated at the right hand of the Father.
He will come again to judge the living and the dead.
Celebrant Do you believe in God the Holy Spirit?
People I believe in the Holy Spirit,
the holy catholic Church,
the communion of saints,
the forgiveness of sins,
the resurrection of the body,
and the life everlasting.

Then, like concentric circles radiating out from the center, the Covenant moves from the base camp to the world.

Celebrant	Will you continue in the apostles' teaching and fellowship, in the breaking of bread, and in the prayers?
People	I will, with God's help.
Celebrant	Will you persevere in resisting evil, and, whenever you fall into sin, repent and return to the Lord?
People	I will, with God's help. (BCP, 304)

These first two questions spell out the essential role of the base camp in the life of the hikers. For the hikers, life in that community is crucial for their journey—their ministry in daily life. The hikers depend on the congregation for their worship and nurture. "No man is an island," John Donne said. No Christian can be a Christian alone, apart from the body of Christ.

A county attorney who is a member of St. Paul's Episcopal Church in Richmond, Virginia, reflected:

> On Sundays, just being in the presence of each of you sharing the sacraments is both calming and renewing. The sense of community . . . uplifts me and supports me for the sometimes ugly conflict inherent in the political world. Our collective church community gives each of us the grace to stretch ourselves at work to be more fully in touch with spiritual values. I am motivated by the example set by other parishioners whose work proclaims Christ every day.[14]

For radical sending, a congregation needs first to examine and then to prioritize its liturgical, formation, pastoral care, and communications programs as to how they provide support for its hikers as they journey beyond the church doors:

- How are its teaching, fellowship, and prayers preparing its hikers for their primary ministry in their world of daily living?
- How is its Eucharist truly "food for the journey"?
- How does its worship both nurture and challenge?
- How is it a resource for reconciliation when the hiker falls short in daily life?

It is one thing to profess our faith standing among other Christians in a church building on a Sunday. It is totally different to live into that faith the other six days of the week in those other buildings we inhabit. That is why what happens on Sunday is so important. It is there in the congregation that the disciples are equipped for the challenges encountered during those other six days.

The Covenant continues with a shift to the life of the hikers outside the congregation—in their world of home, job, school, leisure, community, and wider world.

Celebrant Will you proclaim by word and example the Good News of God in Christ?
People I will, with God's help.
Celebrant Will you seek and serve Christ in all persons, loving your neighbor as yourself?
People I will, with God's help.
Celebrant Will you strive for justice and peace among all people, and respect the dignity of every human being?
People I will, with God's help. (BCP, 305)

A manager of a county community corrections program, also a member of St. Paul's Episcopal Church in Richmond reflected:

One statement from the Baptismal Covenant has had special emphasis for me: "I will respect the dignity of every human being." It is a core value. . . . To be effective in working with mandated clients, people from all walks of life, it helps to look for the human potential, each person's strengths and who they are, not just their problems or what they have done.[15]

Verna Dozier states it clearly:

If I believe that there is a loving God, who has created me and wants me to be part of a people who will carry the good news of the love of that God to the world, what difference does that make when I go to my office at nine o'clock Monday morning? What difference does it make in my office that I believe there is a loving God, that God loves me, and that God loves all human beings exactly as that God loves me? What different kinds of decisions do I make? What am I called to do in that office?[16]

This is the essence of discipleship. This is where the rubber meets the road, where the action is—in the daily life of the baptized where they meet and celebrate and struggle, where all the nurturing and preparation pays off in ministry. In boardrooms and bedrooms, on firing lines and assembly lines, among legislators and landscapers, in courts of law and on tennis courts, in kitchens and kindergartens, in repair shops and coffee shops, among artists and architects, in hospitals and hotels—wherever the *laos*, the people of God are living and working and playing. Quite a ministry!

And in that world of daily life, the laity carry out the functions of bishop, priest, and deacon. The teacher *oversees* a classroom day-by-day (the bishop's function). The parent and the office worker on occasion *bless* and *affirm*, *forgive* and *reconcile* (a priest's function). And, at their best, the waiter or the manager provides *servant* leadership (the deacon's function). The ordained carry out these functions in the ordered life of the church; the laity carry them out in their daily lives.

What a calling, what a vocation, what a ministry! Those empowering words belong to all the people of God. Yet they are far too often reserved for the ordained and perhaps a select group of laypersons, usually in the helping professions. We seem to be reluctant to recognize that the laity are continuously doing ministry. The church needs to catch up and to affirm it.

From the commissioning to the job description, and now to our marching orders: the radical sending, the Dismissal.

The Hikers' Marching Orders

Jesus was quite clear with his followers: "You are the salt of the earth. . . . You are the light of the world" (Matt. 5:13–14). As followers of Jesus, we are not free to exist for our own selves—we are sent out to have an impact on our surroundings—like salt and light. We are to transform our environment.

St. Teresa of Ávila, a sixteenth-century Spanish mystic, wrote:

Christ has no body now on earth but yours; no hands but yours, no feet but yours. Yours are the eyes through which the compassion of Christ must look out on the world. Yours are the feet with which He is to go about doing good. Yours are the hands with which He is to bless His people.

Teresa understands "clothing ourselves with Christ" to be a matter of becoming *alter Christi*, "other Christs," in the world, so that the faithful serve as Christ's very eyes and ears and presence among the people. Hence, at the end of the Episcopal liturgy, come our marching orders:

> And now Father, *send us out* to do the work you have given us to do, to love and serve you as faithful witnesses of Christ our Lord. . . . Let us *go forth* into the world, rejoicing in the power of the Spirit. (BCP, 366)

The liturgy is clear that the work of Christian living is not limited to the worship experience; instead, we are commissioned to use the provisioning that worship provides to sustain us in our true calling, our work "out there" in the world.

Our challenge, then, is to engage in liturgy as the life-giving enterprise it is intended to be, so that we might not only "become what we receive,"[17] as John H. McKenna expresses it, but also that we might share with the world at large, in our daily lives, all that God has so bountifully provided. When the words and actions are truly life-giving, their power cannot be contained inside the building. When the liturgy comes to life, the liturgy becomes connected to life. When the liturgy becomes life-giving, it connects with real life.

Consequently, the sending or Dismissal after the worship is most compelling when it is the culmination of all that has gone before it—praise, prayer, exhortation, communion, homily, and testimony. How we use worship to feed and sustain the faithful is important. But how we send the faithful out to do the work God has given us to do is the hallmark of transformational worship. Our time inside the church building bears fruit when we carry the message into our Monday-through-Sunday lives. If we get the Dismissal right, we get everything right, and "make the whole world Eucharist."[18]

Dr. Seuss, an unexpected resource for Christian doctrine, put it this way in *Oh, the Places You'll Go!*:

> You're off to Great Places!
> Today is your day!
> Your mountain is waiting.
> So . . . get on your way![19]

As Christ ascended, the "men in white" in Acts 1 asked the disciples, "Why do you stand looking up toward heaven?" We're sent out into the world for a reason. As a preacher has put it, "Jesus has left the building—and we will find him out there on the streets." Lutherans refer to the concluding hymn as the "Sending Song."

Along with receiving food for our journey, the most important thing about going to church on Sunday is *leaving.* After all, God has much for us to do and we need to be about it. Go!

Thanks be to God!

GOING FORTH

1. *For noticing or sharing with others:* What idea or thought in this chapter caught your imagination, surprised you, challenged your assumptions, inspired you, raised a question, gave you hope, cautioned you, or opened a new perspective? How does that insight relate to your life as a sent Christian?

2. *For analysis:* How does your faith community serve as your base camp?

3. *For reflection:* When, outside of church, do you think about your weekly worship experience? What does that thinking lead to?

4. *For discussion or discernment:* What in your worship experience might need to change in order to send you out as Christ's ambassador?

5. *For action:* Invite your pastor to have a bag lunch with you where you work. As part of the conversation, share the connection between your faith and your work. If you are the pastor, invite yourself to have a bag lunch with one or more of your members and ask them to share their faith/work connection. See appendix C: Field Trips for potential discussion possibilities. Consider referring to the base camp metaphor as you talk. (A PowerPoint presentation about the base camp is available at www.RadicalSending.com.)

So I Send You

As the Father has sent me, so I send you.

(JOHN 20:21)

Jesus, as recorded in the four Gospels, has a good bit to say about going out and being sent. He is quite clear that he himself is sent from the Father—God has dispatched him on a mission. His references to himself and to his purpose, particularly in the final discourse in John's Gospel (chapters 14–17) are repeatedly linked to "him who sent me." In that final discourse, Jesus focuses intently on the command to love, reminding his disciples that they are to continue living in intimate relationship with the Living God. They are to live the life he has taught and modeled for them, even after he is no longer living with them—no matter where they find themselves. Jesus is quite clear: "As the Father has sent me, so I send you."

Understanding Ourselves as "Sent"

For much of its history, the Church has understood a major part of its work as "missions," and its role as sending missionaries to Christianize the world. Theologian David J. Bosch identified a shift in thinking among missiologists during the latter half of the twentieth century toward describing that sending ("mission") as "not primarily an activity of the church, but an attribute of God. God is a missionary God." Bosch goes on to say, "There is church because there is mission, not vice versa. To participate in mission is to participate in the movement of God's love toward people, since God is a fountain of sending love."[20] As some have said, "God's church doesn't have a mission; God's mission has a church."

Our baptism affirms that, as the Book of Common Prayer phrases it, we Christians are "marked as Christ's own, forever." The Christ that dwells in us not only has been sent, and is sent, but desires to be sent and to send others. Being followers of Christ's way means participating in the mission, living an incarnational practice that recognizes God at work in the world about us and propels us to participate in it. Where we perceive God in action, we are called to join in the work that God is up to. Understanding ourselves as sent by God enlists us in the *missio dei*, "God's sending." When we choose to live our Christianity in this way, anywhere we find ourselves we can choose to participate in God's work of reconciliation. In the words of Erasmus, "Bidden or unbidden, God is present,"[21] and our recognition of that presence confirms our commissioning to join God at work.

To use the hiker metaphor, any trail we choose to walk and any mountain where we trek can offer the potential for engaging us in mission, if we have eyes to see.

A Story of Sending

In Luke 10—a story echoed in both Matthew and Mark—Jesus sends six dozen or so of his followers on a trek, two by two, hiking the metaphorical mountains "where he himself intended to go" (v. 1). He offered specific instructions:

> It's time for you 70 to go. I'm sending you out *armed with vulnerability*, like lambs walking into a pack of wolves. Don't bring a wallet. Don't carry a backpack. I don't even want you to wear sandals. Walk along *barefoot, quietly*, without stopping for small talk. When you enter a house seeking lodging, say, "Peace on this house!" If a child of peace— one who welcomes God's message of peace—is there, your peace will rest on him. If not, don't worry; nothing is wasted. Stay where you're welcomed. *Become part of the family*, eating and drinking whatever they give you. You're My workers, and you deserve to be cared for. Again, don't go from house to house, but settle down in a town and eat whatever they serve you. Heal the sick and say to the townspeople, "The kingdom of God has come near to you." (Luke 10:3–9, *The Voice*)

It's easy to forget that these "hikers" were sent out to bring Good News, long before the story as we know it had unfolded. Jesus had not yet been tried, crucified, and raised. The Good News, in addition to healing, was essentially God's message of peace: God is here. Our twenty-first century ideas of God's Good News—sanctification, atonement, justification by faith, Christ's victory over death, and more—were not even in the picture. No one has a copy of a sermon that was preached by these early hikers—who almost certainly offered their message within the intimacy of a small group, and whose way of life was their most powerful witness. Perhaps their message spoke of God's acceptance and healing and of the transforming relationship found among their community of believers.

Look at the excitement of their return from their expedition: "The seventy returned with joy, saying, 'Lord, in your name even the demons submit to us!'" (Luke 10:17). Sent out empty-handed and vulnerable by Jesus, the hikers discovered their effectiveness, their agency, and the transformative power of their message. They returned with joy, to share the stories of their hike with their fellow travelers at their "base camp." They had been equipped and provisioned for their journey in ways they had not previously imagined, and their work had borne much good fruit. That common experience—lived out two-by-two—began forging an extended community that would one day transform the world.

A congregation seeking to embody such a missional God can take heart from the example of these early disciples. The joy in their journey—and the electrifying, transformational realization of God's power acting through them—came not from experiences of worshipping together. It came, instead, from following The Way on the way. The hikers' experiences of God out in the field fueled their faith, so that they brought that energy back to the base camp, to refresh and renew other hikers.

Disciples and Apostles

In popular vernacular, many use the terms "disciple" and "apostle" as practically interchangeable, designating New Testament followers of Jesus. Few in the twenty-first century would use either term to describe themselves, except perhaps as a member of a particular denomination.

"Disciple" comes to us from the Latin for pupil, the same root that gives us "discipline." Much of the church's teaching ministry—schools, Sunday schools, Bible translation, and curricula of all kinds—arises from the desire to teach the faith to its pupils. Matthew 28:18–20 (often termed "The Great Commission") speaks of "making disciples of all nations." The church has traditionally focused on sending missionaries as teachers of the tenets of the Christian faith, often using memorization of Scripture, creeds, and catechisms as principal tools for "making disciples."

More recent scholarship points to the Great Commission as calling Christians not so much to "make disciples" as to "disciple"—that is, to walk alongside others in the practice of The Way of Jesus. That casts the Great Commission in the spirit of Matthew 11:29: "Take my yoke upon you and learn from me," evoking the farmer's practice of yoking an undisciplined young ox with a steadier, more mature partner so that the younger will learn to work more effectively.

The term "apostle" comes from the Greek, meaning "one who is sent." In the four Gospels, the NRSV translation restricts this term to The Twelve. In Christian tradition, Mary Magdalene has been named "the apostle to the apostles," and in Paul's letters he confers that title upon himself and even on some among the community of faith, such as Andronicus and Junia in Romans 16:7.

In *Transforming Congregations for the Future*, author and educator Loren Mead calls on the church to recognize its role in making both disciples and apostles. He recognizes the changing understanding of mission, as laity take on new roles in the church.

> The story of Jesus leads us to become disciples and apostles carrying forth the kind of good news that Jesus modeled—a good news that is profoundly contextual, touching the different kinds of pain present at any place; a good news that comes in many shapes and sizes; a good news that always leaves the recipient free to accept or reject it. Congregations, then, are about helping us all become disciples and apostles.
>
> The root of it all is transformation. The transformation of each of us into a disciple whose life has been touched and shaped by Jesus' good news. The transformation of each of us into a special part of the apostolate Jesus is calling into being to proclaim his reign over all.[22]

The teaching and discipling functions of the church—known as formation—bear fruit in the sending of believers as apostles into the world, to be *alter Christi*—"other Christs"—representing the incarnate, reconciling presence of God.

Dwight Zscheile, an Episcopal priest and educator, describes this interaction of discipleship and apostleship.

If the emergence of Christendom in the late patristic and early medieval period brought a turn inward in Christian spiritual formation, away from the world, today's post-Christian cultural context invites us to reimagine formation in deep engagement with the world. . . . Christians in ordinary congregations must innovate new ways of living as disciples. Now is a time in which the whole church would benefit from the mutual sharing of lived stories, parables, and illustrations of vital and risky Christian witness and service. Every context is different, yet such stories are integral to enriching our communal imagination for mission.[23]

Susan Hope quotes from the *Mission-Shaped Church* report produced by the Church of England in describing the church's new role: "The defining word for the Church and its mission has changed from 'come' to 'go'; and not just geographically, but going to be with people how they are, 'connecting with their lifestyles, values, networks, culture.'"[24]

Congregations have an essential role in discipleship, especially in the work to equip the church to be a "going concern." In the process of forming Christians, congregations can foster the awareness that all people are commissioned by their baptism to carry the message of God's Good News into the community, beyond the walls of the church building. Each person, having been formed in faith by the congregation, leaves the church base camp as an apostle, sent out into the world. As in the Luke 10 story, hikers return with the Good News of what they have experienced—the stories of transformation, their own and others'—lived through their "vital and risky Christian witness and service," as Zscheile describes it. And those stories of the transformational power of God's Good News in action work to enliven the congregation to its true calling.

In the words of theologian Lesslie Newbigin, "We are chosen in order to be sent."[25] And we are sent in order both to share the Good News and to bring our own Good News stories back to the base camp, even if they may involve pain and suffering. We are in that apostolic succession of those who are sent.

The Radical Way

"Radical" is not one of those words that Christian communities often use to describe themselves. It comes to us from the Latin word for "root," and it describes something fundamental. In recent years it's come to be associated with "beyond the pale," "far out," or even "crazy," from the endless news reports of "radical extremists." Stephanie Spellers's use of the term "radical welcome" grew out of her need to describe the broad spectrum of practices churches might embrace to model the creative, far-reaching inclusivity that Christ calls us to, the very root of our Christian community. We're inclined to shy away from such a hard-edged descriptor for Christian action—but that is the very dynamic that Christ is calling us to adopt.

Jesuit communities, basing their life together on the practices of Ignatius of Loyola, maintain that there are four life postures required in order to make life-giving decisions in a group process of discerning God's purpose in a particular time and place. Each person participating is called to be

- Ready to move in any direction that God wants, therefore radically free;
- Open to sharing all that God has given him or her, therefore radically generous;
- Willing to suffer if God's will requires it, therefore radically patient;
- Questing for union with God in prayer, therefore radically spiritual.[26]

Those radical attributes—freedom, generosity, patience, and spirituality—are the very soil that nurtures both "radical welcome" and "radical sending." The practices of community discernment and community action equip us to be present and engaged with those we encounter, whether inside the church or in the wider community. And those practices form us to be "the sent ones," who carry the radical Good News of God's unfailing presence among us.

Returning to the roots of our faith—the radical, transformational practices of Jesus—is the challenge and the reward of understanding ourselves as sent by Christ, just as the Father sent him, to go and serve as his apostles in our daily lives. It is just such a mission that calls the baptized to radically redefine their lives as Christians, to see their calling to be the *alter Christi* in their worlds of work, family, community, and school—and the local church is there as a base camp to equip and affirm and encourage them in their apostleship.

GOING FORTH

1. *For noticing or sharing with others*: What idea or thought in this chapter caught your imagination, surprised you, challenged your assumptions, inspired you, raised a question, gave you hope, cautioned you, or opened a new perspective? How does that insight relate to your life as a sent Christian?

2. *For analysis:* For what purposes does your faith community send people out? How are those efforts communicated?

3. *For reflection:* Aside from church, when have you been sent out to accomplish something? (In your work? In your family? In a game or contest?) What equipped you to make your best effort trying to accomplish it? How is that related to your faith in daily life?

4. *For discussion or discernment:* Where do you see God at work in your neighborhood, town, or city? What might you need from your faith community to be equipped to join in that work—to be an apostle, one who is sent?

5. *For action:* Choose one of the "sending" Scriptures cited in this chapter, and use it as an affirmation for the coming week. (Post it on your mirror, write yourself an e-mail, or enter it on your calendar.) What do you notice?

A Timeless
Expression

In all I do this day
In all I think or say
Father be with me all the way.
In all my work and all my deeds
In all I learn, in all my needs
Christ, go before me, the One who leads.
In my work as I do my best
In all that puts me to the test,
Spirit, help, and grant me rest.

DAVID ADAM, *POWER LINES*

The practice of regarding all of life, even the mundane, as sacred is not a new practice among Christians. Many believe that Christianity in the British Isles has been rooted for nearly two thousand years in a profoundly incarnational understanding of the holiness of daily work. The prayer lives of Celtic Christians are profound expressions of the presence of God in all of life.

May there always be work for your hands to do;
May your purse always hold a coin or two;
May the sun always shine on your windowpane;
May a rainbow be certain to follow each rain;
May the hand of a friend always be near you;
May God fill your heart with gladness to cheer you.

and may you be in heaven a half hour
before the devil knows you're dead.[27]

Such wisdom and humor comes from an unknown Celtic Christian who traces his roots to the first Christian missionaries that arrived in Ireland and Scotland before the fourth century CE. Those pioneers found there a Celtic people deeply committed to the sacredness of all of the creation. Those native Druids practiced a pantheistic religion that worshipped many gods—all connected with the creation around them. They had sacred wells and sacred stone pillars, a deep respect for the cycle of plant and flower life from seed to nurture to blossom to wilting to death to rebirth in the spring. Tapping such rich spiritual resources, those early Christian missionaries—Patrick, Columba, Brigid, and Brendan—translated the wells into baptism, the pillars into crosses, the planting cycle into the death and resurrection of Christ.

Notice how St. Patrick (390–461 CE) in his creed integrates Druidic polytheism into the celebration of the one God of all creation:

Our God, God of all men,
God of heaven and earth, seas and rivers,
God of sun and moon, of all the stars,
God of high mountains and lowly valleys,
God over heaven, and in heaven, and under heaven.
He has a dwelling in heaven and earth and sea
And in all things that are in them.
He inspires all things, he quickens all things,
He is over all things, he supports all things.
He makes the light in the sun to shine,
He surrounds the moon and the stars,
He has made wells in the arid earth,
Placed dry islands in the sea.
He has a Son coeternal with himself . . .
And the Holy Spirit breathes in them;
Not separate are Father and Son and Holy Spirit.[28]

Out of that great respect and celebration of God's gifts in creation comes the Christian's response to God's immanence in God's world: the call for stewardship of creation and for one's vocation in daily life. The big book was the creation, the little book the Bible. Learn from both, the Celtic Christians proclaimed.

That sense of the sacredness of daily life is expressed in this prayer:

> The Sacred Three be over me
> With my working hands this day
> With the people on my way
> With the labor and the toil
> With the land and with the soil
> With the tools that I take
> With the things that I make
> With the thoughts of my mind
> With the sharing of humankind
> With the love of my heart
> With each one that plays a part
> The Sacred Three be over me
> The blessing of the Trinity.[29]

Esther de Waal, a scholar in the Benedictine and Celtic traditions, is an Anglican laywoman living in the Welsh-English borderlands where she grew up. She explains:

> The sense of God informs daily life and transforms it, so that any moment, any object, any job of work, can become the time and place for an encounter with God. It is ultimately a question of vision, of seeing. So the Celtic approach to God opens up a world in which nothing is too common to be exalted and nothing is so exalted that it cannot be made common.[30]

Living into the sacredness of every element of her life, the Celtic wife/mother would rise before dawn, before the rest of the family. As she kindled the fire at the very start of her day, she would call forth God's blessings upon its light and its cooking usefulness and its warmth, from which radiated the love of God, a presence that she continued to experience in her chores the rest of the day.

> I will kindle my fire this morning
> In presence of the holy angels of heaven. . . .
> Without malice, without jealousy, without envy,
> Without fear, without terror of any one under the sun,
> But the Holy Son of God to shield me.
>
> God, kindle Thou in my heart within
> A flame of love to my neighbour,

> To my foe, to my friend, to my kindred all,
> To the brave, to the knave, to the thrall,
> O Son of the loveliest Mary.[31]

As she moves through her day, she does so with the consciousness of God's blessing from the loom to milking to childcare to the day's end at the hearth and the bed. "The circle of belonging." Because Celtic spirituality is so focused on the sacredness of daily life, there are thousands of "blessings" within the tradition because God is so incarnate, so immanent. This sense of blessing is calling upon God to sanctify every aspect of life, even its most mundane aspects, like this ancient milking prayer of our wife/mother:

> Bless, O God, my little cow,
> Bless, O God, my desire;
> Bless Thou my partnership
> And the milking of my hands, O God.
> Bless, O God, each teat,
> Bless, O God, each drop,
> That goes into my pitcher, O God.[32]

And so to bed at night:

> I AM lying down to-night,
> With Father, with Son,
> With the Spirit of Truth,
> Who shield me from harm.[33]

In similar ways Celtic Christians have prayed over the centuries about the sacredness of everyday life, developing traditions distinct from the rest of Western Roman Christendom. Rather than the more Western focus on the second and third chapters of Genesis (Adam and Eve and sin), Celtic Christianity's primary focus was on God's creation (Genesis 1), wherein all of the creation is declared very good and humankind is created in God's image. As all the creation is God's and humankind is called to good stewardship, so everyday life is seen as sacred.

Of central importance in those early days was the monastic community at Iona, an island off the western coast of Scotland. Exiled from Ireland, Columba (521–597 CE) and twelve other monks founded the monastery. Over the next several centuries it played a significant role in the conversion of Scotland and beyond to the Celtic spirit.

Celtic Christianity flourished, until the Council of Whitby (664 CE), which gave authority to the church in Rome over the much smaller, but vibrant, church in Ireland, Wales, and Scotland.

That Celtic spirit may have gone underground, but it never was lost in the tradition of Ireland and Scotland. It surfaces in poems like this from the seventh century, which is also found in many hymnals, including *The Hymnal 1982* (#488):

> Be thou my vision, O Lord of my heart;
> all else be nought to me, save that thou art. . . .

In 1938 George MacLeod, a Scots Presbyterian, reestablished the Iona Community. This community, together with one in Northumbria, England, is now a leading force in the present-day Celtic Christian revival and resurgence with its renewed focus on reverence for the creation and derivative from that, the sacredness of everyday life. Modern pilgrims to Iona often refer to it as a "thin place," a place where they literally experience the close proximity of heaven and earth, the eternal in the temporal. There is a Celtic saying that heaven and earth are only three feet apart, but in thin places that distance is even shorter. Translate that to everyday life and any place, any moment, any person can be a "thin place."

Among modern Celtic Christians is the Irish poet John O'Donohue (1956–2008), who reflects on the sacredness of work, "May you experience each day as a sacred gift woven around the heart of wonder."[34] He offers this prayer:

> May the light of your soul bless the work you do
> with the secret love and warmth of your heart;
> May you see in what you do the beauty of your own soul;
> May the sacredness of your work bring healing,
> light and renewal to those who work with you
> and to those who see and receive your work;
> May your work never weary you;
> May it release within you wellsprings of refreshment,
> inspiration and excitement;
> May you be present in what you do.[35]

And if that sounds a bit idealistic, an ancient Irish prayer provides a balance:

> May you see God's light on the path ahead
> When the road you walk is dark.
> May you always hear,
> Even in your hour of sorrow,
> The gentle singing of the lark.
> When times are hard may hardness
> Never turn your heart to stone,
> May you always remember
> when the shadows fall—
> You do not walk alone.[36]

As the above examples demonstrate, within the Celtic prayers and poems there is a repetitive rhythm of key words, such as bless, may, God, and Christ, for the prayers were often chanted.

Mary Earle, a writer, spiritual director, retreat leader, and Episcopal priest, has studied Celtic practice extensively. She teaches:

> These prayers lead us to remember that the work we do, "the handling of our hands," is done in partnership with the God who creates us and sets daily tasks before us. Our work is our means of making visible the bonds that unite us, and our means of honoring one another in God. The daily labor in which we engage, no matter how seemingly humdrum, is the very place in which we love both God and neighbor, in which we may offer ourselves for the common good.[37]

All of life is sacramental—outward and visible signs of inward and spiritual grace—including life on the job, in the home, in the community, and in the church. Can we open ourselves to experience that inward and spiritual grace any time, any place? The corrections official, loan officer, volunteer little league coach, contract lawyer, high school math teacher, and the stay-at-home mom all may experience the holy in their vocations. "May the Christ in me meet and greet the Christ in the other," as the mantra goes.

For our modern life, Celtic Christianity witnesses to the sacredness of everyday living. Its strong sense of God's presence in the creation and in the midst of daily life provides a beacon for each of us in our journey in Christ. It is a tradition that sees the holy in the common and the common in the holy, where nothing is so ordinary that it lacks God's real presence. It calls us to intentionality, to an increasing awareness of how sacred every moment, every thing, every person is in God's eyes. So this prayer attributed to St. Patrick encourages us to that intentionality:

> As I arise today,
> may the strength of God pilot me,
> the power of God uphold me,
> the wisdom of God guide me.
> May the eye of God look before me,
> the ear of God hear me,
> the word of God speak for me.
> May the hand of God protect me,
> the way of God lie before me,
> the shield of God defend me,
> the host of God save me.
> May Christ shield me today.[38]

We are reminded of the radical sending to "go into our worlds of home, work, and community rejoicing in the power of the Spirit." As we go forth, let this traditional Irish blessing be ours as well:

> Work like you don't need the money.
> Love like you've never been hurt.
> Dance like nobody's watching.
> Sing like nobody's listening.
> Live like it's Heaven on Earth.[39]

GOING FORTH

1. *For noticing or sharing with others:* What idea or thought in this chapter caught your imagination, surprised you, challenged your assumptions, inspired you, raised a question, gave you hope, cautioned you, or opened a new perspective? How does that insight relate to your life as a sent Christian?

2. *For analysis:* What in the Celtic practice of Christianity do you think inspired so many prayers focused on such ordinary aspects of daily life?

3. *For reflection:* What everyday task might you offer to God in prayer as you do it? How might that offering shape your feelings about that task?

4. *For discussion or discernment:* Where in your daily life do you find it hardest to make the faith connection? Who or what might help you catch sight of God in that seemingly God-forsaken place or situation?

5. *For action:* Try writing a one sentence prayer that connects with an aspect of your daily life. Recite it daily for a week, and then share it with someone or journal about your experience.

In Their Own Words

The housemaid on her knees scrubbing the floor is
doing a work as pleasing in the sight of Almighty God
as the priest on his knees before the altar saying Mass.

MARTIN LUTHER, "AN OPEN LETTER TO THE CHRISTIAN NOBILITY"

The Celtic view of the wholeness of creation, explored in the previous chapter, has persisted over centuries. As two Episcopalians, we take note of "radical sending" congregations that are beginning to spring up across the church, contemporary expressions of a Christianity that is integral to daily life. In particular, our Lutheran, Mennonite, and Roman Catholic brothers and sisters are making strides in creating base camp congregations. In this chapter we take a look at thoughts and visions from other currents in the great Christian river. We hope that you will find resonance with your own experience and inspiration for your congregation to discern its own expression of "radical sending."

Our Lutheran Connection

A Lutheran pastor quotes Luther as saying, "Whatever it is [that] people are doing is holy work." Keith Graber Miller explains:

> [Luther] maintained that all stations in life in which it is possible to live honestly are divine vocations. Those stations included those which are to be found in the family (husband, father, wife, mother, child, friend); those which belonged to the economic order (shopkeeper, milkmaid, laborer); and those which are part of political life (queen, governor or subject). All of these estates, Luther believed, are "masks" of God, faces through which the work of God in human life can be revealed.[40]

Jack Fortin, pastor and professor at Augsburg College, quotes Philipp Melancthon, a reformer and a collaborator with Luther, as saying, "It would be a shame to be known by where we gather and not where we scatter."

Craig L. Nessan, pastor and professor at Wartburg Theological Seminary, points out how Luther's vision has gone unfulfilled, lamenting, "Whereas the Reformation theologians sought to reconfigure the late medieval priesthood as the priesthood of all believers, the practice of the Reformation churches has never delivered on the potency of this proposal."[41]

Richard Bruesehoff, Lutheran pastor and former Director for Lifelong Learning for his denomination, underscored the need for a paradigm shift in clergy/laity relations:

> The role of pastor/priest really needs to change. It is obviously no longer the role of doing ministry to/for everyone in the congregation. It becomes far more the role of equipping and supporting those who are doing their ministry in the world. . . . The problem being addressed has two fronts: clergy who feel the need to be in control/to own ministry AND laity who have gotten used to clergy who provide ministry to them (kind of a consumer model) and really kind of like it that way.[42]

In recent days, Lutherans have been breathing new life into Luther's dream as envisioned by Fortin:

> I believe that there is great potential for congregations to offer just the nurture and support that help people live out their faith in their daily lives in their workplaces, the family and the community. I believe that congregations are the best places for God's people to be inspired and equipped to live out their callings each day. I envision congregations as places where people gather, are cared for, equipped and validated for their everyday mission and ministry, and then set free to serve God in their many vocational settings. Our need for a place to belong and to make a difference in the world can come together in the congregation.[43]

During a conference call with the authors on January 20, 2015, Fortin recalled a conversation he had with Peter Drucker, best known for his management leadership books. Fortin quoted Drucker as saying, "The future still goes back to the congregation, where formation shapes and gives energy so that people have courage to take authentic action in the workplace." Fortin said he relies on humble "friendly experiments" arising out of congregations to model the hope he sees embodied in Luther's "priesthood of all believers."

Lutherans are continuing to reclaim Luther's dream. In preparation for their 2016 Churchwide Assembly, the Covenant Cluster Taskforce on Lay Theological Education circulated a model resolution for synod assemblies to consider, which included this key provision supported by a number of enabling clauses:

> Resolved, That we call upon congregations to foster Christian vocation by encouraging and equipping people, from children to adults, to discern and claim their call to speak and live the faith in their daily lives through their many varied forms of service with our neighbors in the family, the workplace, and in civil society.[44]

In its e-mail distributing the model resolution on February 9, 2015 (which you can read in its entirety at www.RadicalSending.com), Craig L. Nessan, a member of the task force, wrote:

> We believe the Life of Faith Initiative will transform the shape of the church's mission in our time by reclaiming the promise of the universal priesthood of all believers. We invite you to read, study, and affirm the attached model resolution about a Life of Faith Initiative in the congregations, synods, and diverse ministries of the ELCA. We encourage you to promote this effort by submitting this resolution for adoption by your 2015 Synod Assembly to make this focus a priority for our life together as church.[45]

Seeking to Support Equipping Pastors

In 2011, Lutheran pastor and educator Dwight DuBois initiated a series of small group meetings focused on the ministry of all the baptized in their daily lives with Lutheran pastors in Iowa. He tells the story:

> It was a simple request: a nearby pastor suggested that we find a few pastors who would be interested in gathering for a book study on what it means to be "an equipping pastor," that is, what it means to be pastors who see their job principally in terms of preparing and empowering people for ministry in their everyday lives. I was immediately interested and started looking for a book that would serve as the centerpiece for such a study group.[46]

When DuBois sent out invitations to 139 Lutheran pastors in the Southeastern Iowa Synod, expecting six to twelve to reply, he was overwhelmed to find that more than fifty wanted in. Many expressed deep interest: "I have a passion for this topic." "It's a key area of congregational health." "There is a crying need to work on this." His process was a series of small group meetings. In the course of those meetings, some core questions arose:

- What does it mean to be an equipping pastor?
- How is that different from what most pastors were trained to be and do?
- What implication does this hold for program, staff, structure, and day-to-day operation of a congregation?
- How does one shift from being a "pastoral" or "program" pastor to being an equipping pastor?
- How might we describe, empower, and support pastors who see their calling in terms of equipping members for ministry in their everyday lives?[47]

As the pastors wrestled with what it means to be an equipping pastor, some problems surfaced: the reality that the power of "the priesthood of all believers" has not been unleashed; the "inward-facing" focus of seminary education; church structures that work against recognizing ministry outside the church; the wide-spread perception that "ministry is the pastor's job"; people are leaving the church because "what happens there has no connection to my life"; and "people are already doing ministry, they just don't know it."[48]

The report also offers strong affirmations for pastors seeking to become more skillful in equipping their congregations. DuBois quotes a Church of the Brethren judicatory leader: "We are a sent people. We don't wait for someone to send us out and then we go; we're already there."[49] Echoing Luther's statement, "Whatever it is [that] people are doing is holy work," DuBois offers the observation that the people of God are at work for the sake of the world:

> Ministry happens in the farm field, where food is grown so that people might be fed. Ministry happens in classrooms, where children and adults receive education necessary for their welfare and for the sake of the world. Ministry happens when a parent changes a diaper, clothes and feeds, shelters and raises their child. Ministry happens when an adult child cares for their aging parent. Ministry happens in the workplace where products are produced, where countless decisions are made, where people and all creation are protected and served.[50]

Ministry in the world is, after all, God's purpose for the church. DuBois says:

> One pastor cited author Kelly Fryer who says that ministry in daily life is not a matter of "taking Jesus out there," but joining God out there, who is already at work. Another added, "God is everywhere; God is equipping all the time." And another said, "So maybe we go to a member and ask, 'What is God doing in the insurance business these days?'"[51]

DuBois quotes one pastor as summarizing, "The central task of an equipping pastor is to attend to and name the ministry you see or hear from the members. It's not a program to teach them how to do it, it's helping them see that they are doing ministry."[52] A few pages later, DuBois urges:

> This doesn't need to be another program, something "more" that people can, should, or ought to do. As one theologian in the missional church movement said, our task is to "guide people to identify God's calling, to recognize the gifts and opportunities they have, to provide them the biblical and theological training to incarnate the gospel in their particular fields, and then to commission them to that ministry."[53]

The pastor's task is to provide a place where people can articulate the ministry that they are already doing. DuBois cites Elton Trueblood:

> Pastors are not called to get people to assist them with their ministry; rather, the pastor is called to assist the people, the laity, with *their* ministry both in the church and in the world.[54]

DuBois quotes one pastor as saying, "This all starts with our attitude—that we value what people do and we encourage their ministry." Another pastor went on to offer an interesting mental image: "I find myself wanting to walk my people to the door. How do we get the good news that we celebrate here out of the church and into the community?"[55]

Reimagining Luther's Vision

Craig L. Nessan, quoted above, asks his readers to understand *diakonia* (usually interpreted as "service" or "servanthood") as "neighborliness" in reimagining Luther's vision:

In large part, the limitation of Reformation theology in relation to the priesthood of all believers is tied to the continued usage of the term "priesthood" to describe the vocation of the baptized. The metaphor of "priesthood" perpetuates a clerical misunderstanding of Christian vocation in the world, that is, real ministry is what "priests" (clergy) do.[56]

Nessan goes on to offer, in fine Lutheran tradition, twenty theses that "sketch out an alternative theology for the ministry of the baptized in the world under the concept, 'the neighborliness (*diakonia*) of all believers.'"[57] (His unpublished paper "The Neighborliness (*Diakonia*) of All Believers: Toward Reimagining the Universal Priesthood" can be found at www.RadicalSending.com.) Three of these theses read:

7. Shalom ministry—which encompasses peacemaking, social justice, care for creation, and respect for inherent human dignity—is lived out as Christian neighborliness in the four primary arenas in which God has placed us for service to others in this world: (a) family, (b) daily work, (c) religious institutions, and (d) engagement for the common good.

12. The rosters of the Evangelical Lutheran Church in America are each properly oriented in a theology of ministry that gives priority to equipping the baptized for neighborliness in daily life.

14. Ordained ministers serve Word and sacrament through preaching, teaching, worship leadership, and pastoral care, in order that the baptized are set free by the Gospel of Jesus Christ *from* all that holds them captive and free *for* serving the neighbors whom God gives them in the four arenas of daily life.[58]

Judith McWilliams Dickhart, a Lutheran pastor, has written an insightful book: *Church-Going Insider or Gospel-Carrying Outsider.* The heart and essence of her message is shown in this chart (on page 53), where she contrasts two views of a congregation's mission and calls for the change that leads to a Gospel-carrying outsider—a person empowered to function outside the walls of the church as a bearer of God's Good News.[59]

A SUMMARY OF INSIDE/OUTSIDE ASSUMPTIONS

Well-worn assumptions	. . . re-viewed
Congregations should grow in numbers and strength. The greater the number of church members, the wider the knowledge of the Gospel in the community.	**Congregations should carry God's love into the World.** Congregations are "commissioning centers"—one of the means God uses to deliver the Gospel in particular places, in partnership with other groups, and through daily discipleship of members.
Members should go to church regularly. People who really believe the Gospel will express their faith by worshiping weekly and participating in other church activities.	**Members should be the Church always.** People who are baptized will express their faith when they gather with other Christians inside the church and when they use their gifts to serve God in their daily places.
Congregations should draw new persons into membership. If unchurched people would just come into the church building, they would hear the Gospel, enjoy the fellowship, and join the church.	**Congregations should take the "church" to where people are.** Those outside the church need to see the Gospel in everyday places, and hear it shared with everyday words. At some point they may become seekers ready to find a church in which they can learn more.
Congregations need to increase their resources, staff, and programs. To become larger and stronger, churches need to expand worship, education, and program opportunities that require more human, financial, and physical resources.	**Congregations need to equip members to minister in God's World.** Congregations become stronger when they recognize that members are their greatest resource for doing mission, and concentrate on encouraging, equipping, and supporting members in their everyday ministries.

Dickhart creates a similar chart (below), contrasting "new angle" understandings of the roles of laity and clergy with "well-worn assumptions."[60]

THE ROLES OF CLERGY AND LAITY INSIDE AND OUT

Well-worn assumptions	. . . from a new angle
Pastors are in charge of the mission. They are the most knowledgeable and best qualified to set the direction and to call on members to help.	**Laity are equally responsible for the mission.** They are knowledgeable about mission in the world and have the most access to those outside the church.
Pastors are the ministers. Their ordination gives them the authority to minister.	**All Christians are ministers.** Their baptism gives both clergy and laity the authority to minister.
Pastors carry out the congregation's mission with laity support. They are official leaders of congregations and bear primary responsibility for what is accomplished.	**Laypeople carry out the mission with the support of clergy.** They have the most opportunity to deliver God's love in the world, while their pastors teach, encourage, and support them.
Lay members use their gifts primarily in the church's programs. Their gifts are best used in the congregation's ongoing program, which is the main way laity support the mission of the church.	**Lay members use their gifts most often in the daily places.** Their gifts are most often used in their daily places of family, community, and work, which are their main arenas for doing mission.
Pastors are the evangelists who attract outsiders into the church. Clergy are the main reason new people come to church. Their preaching and personal attention turn visitors into members.	**Lay members are the evangelists in whom outsiders see God's love.** Laity represent the church as they express their faith in words and caring deeds during their daily contacts with the unchurched.
Pastors are full-time ministers. Their work for the church goes on twenty-four-hours a day, seven days a week. Laypersons, on the other hand, minister part-time through church programs and charitable activities.	**All Christians minister full-time.** Both pastors and lay members minister inside the church. Both minister on the outside too. Pastors are laypersons in their families and communities.

A Professor's Story

This movement toward reclaiming Luther's concept of "the priesthood of all believers" is not restricted to academicians and theologians. Bob Victorin-Vangerud, a Lutheran professor who teaches philosophy in a community college in Minneapolis, Minnesota, offers an extended reflection on the Sunday-Monday Connection in his own life:

> *How do I live out my baptismal calling in the workplace? To address that question, I want to start with Communion. I teach philosophy in a community college. Philosophers get to ask all kinds of interesting questions, like "What's the meaning of life?" Now in my fifties I think I have figured out what the meaning of life is. That would be "generosity and gratitude." I could point to philosophers who say that kind of thing, but I didn't learn it from them. I learned it from Jesus. As early as I can remember, maybe as early as three or four years after that baptism that called me, I've heard each week how "on the night in which he was betrayed, Jesus took bread, gave thanks, and broke it, and gave it to his disciples."*
>
> *So Jesus was grateful, giving thanks. He demonstrated generosity, giving the bread (and himself) to the people around him. That's the kind of life we are baptized into. It starts with an act of generosity from God and then spreads from there. The proper gratitude for that generosity is to respond in kind, with generosity. And of course this example from Jesus happened on the night in which one of those close to him betrays his trust to the point of death. So we practice generosity not just when we win the lottery . . . but when the ground is disappearing from beneath our feet. . . . The baptismal calling is a calling into a life of radical generosity and gratitude. We talk about grace and love, and that's what I mean when I use those words.*
>
> *So how does that calling play itself out in teaching philosophy? Well, the philosophy part involves, as the ancients say, cultivating wonder. Actually the better translation of their word,* thaumazein, *is "astonishment," even "shock." To cultivate that "astonishment," one often has to question what we assume is true, what we take for granted, or what we doubt but are too afraid to really set aside because of custom or self-protection. So in a world where students are too often trained to go on to fill the halls of acquisition, control, and self-promotion, wonder looks like the opposite of that—generosity and gratitude; wonder trusts the world and trusts the idea, trusts thinking to open things up rather than shut them down, trusts perhaps that the divine wonder is behind our astonishment.*

Then there's the teaching *part of teaching philosophy. When you teach a person, you give them something that, once it is given, can never be taken back. . . . Knowledge is like grace. It is not diminished in the sharing but is instead enhanced, made greater in the movement from "I know" to "we know." I get a paycheck for teaching, but if it were just the money that got me to work each day, I'd find a different job. In my mind I've never really been able to translate what I do in the classroom into the dollars that show up in my bank account. The teaching and the money always seem incommensurable. . . . In the end I teach in gratitude to the people who taught me, who gave me what I didn't even know I wanted until I had received it.*

What difference does baptismal calling make in the way I do my job? Well, I love my students. The baptismal calling is to love everyone, an impossible task, but that's the deal. I love my students. I don't always like them, but I love them. By love I mean cultivating the awareness of the singularity of each student, that each one is unique and unrepeatable and deserves everything I can give him or her and more. That's what we mean, I believe, by the term "the image of God." . . .

My English teacher in college didn't plod through my dull words with me because he had to. He could have corrected my typos, assigned a grade, and been done with it, martini in hand. But he did it; he did it because he wanted to. He cared about this single kid staring blankly at him from the back row of class three times a week. It was an act of love. And I'm grateful.[61]

Our Mennonite Connection

Although our Mennonite brothers and sisters are products of the sixteenth-century Reformation, they put their theological roots firmly in the life, death, and resurrection of Jesus and in the community he established. There are two teachings at the heart of that community's life: Paul's extended metaphor of the body of Christ (1 Cor. 12:12ff) where all share in equal dignity, and the enlightened image of the priesthood of all believers found in 1 Peter 2:9–10. At the center is the vocation of all believers—the call to be disciples of Jesus. Every other "call" stems from that Christ-centered vocation.

Keith Graber Miller, a professor at Goshen College in Goshen, Indiana, offered an overview of the Mennonite perspective on transforming the theology of vocation.[62] He reports that the early Anabaptists-Mennonites took the idea of "call" so seriously that they ruled out jobs in government, commerce, and trade as too prone to evil, and thus,

such jobs were—by Anabaptist theology—on the forbidden list. Menno
Simons (c. 1496–1561), quoting Ecclesiasticus 26:29–27:3, wrote:

> "A merchant can hardly keep from wrongdoing, nor is a tradesman
> innocent of sin. . . . As a stake is driven firmly into a fissure between
> stones, so sin is wedged in between selling and buying." Some mer-
> chants, Simons noted, become thieves, murderers, and holdup men,
> gamblers, betrayers, and brothel keepers, executioners and torment-
> ers, all for the sake of profit.[63]

The center of Mennonite living, therefore, was mainly in agricul-
ture and in crafts, with their products to be traded mainly within their
own community.

As European Mennonites immigrated to North America, they
brought with them some of these prohibitions, but they were tem-
pered by Russian Mennonite immigrants of the late nineteenth and
early twentieth centuries many of whom

> had been entrepreneurs in Russia, running factories, hospitals, and
> institutions for training teachers. . . . In many of these roles, they have
> functioned as essentially self-employed owners—or people who par-
> ticipate in management decisions as quasi-owners—and they have
> been appreciated for their artistry, efficiency, and dependability.
> [This led to] a dramatic shift in Mennonite occupations—from
> small-town crafts and farming to the professions and the office—[that]
> has taken place rather rapidly since the 1950s.[64]

Graber Miller adds that during the second half of the twentieth century, the number of young Mennonites entering professions grew dra-
matically along with the number of different fields they chose to enter.

> By 2006, only twelve percent of U.S. Mennonite adults lived on a
> farm, compared with three times that many in the early 1970s. Dur-
> ing that same period the number of Mennonites in professional and
> technical roles increased rapidly, expanding as these occupational
> roles emerged and went through their own transformations. By 2006,
> forty-one percent of U.S. Mennonites were in managerial and profes-
> sional occupations, and twenty-seven percent were in technical, sales,
> and administrative support roles. The entry of massive numbers of
> Mennonite women into the workforce marked yet another dramatic
> transformation in the North American occupational landscape in the
> last fifty years. By 2006, only eight percent of U.S. Mennonites identi-
> fied themselves as housewives/homemakers.[65]

What is significant about this urban shift is that the deeply held sense of Christian vocation has continued at the core of the Mennonite community. Graber Miller makes the point that despite the changed context, Mennonites' theology of vocation remains vibrant:

> Clearly, North American Mennonites in the twenty-first century live in a very different context than that of their sixteenth century forebears. Mennonites in North America are not persecuted for their faith, nor do they need to provide theological arguments for a withdrawal on which their survival depended. . . . Today Mennonites have full access to professions from which they were previously barred, and they are moving eagerly into these occupations and others that simply did not exist in earlier centuries.
>
> At the same time, however, sixteenth century Anabaptists and twenty-first century North American Mennonites do share some theological and ethical continuity in their understandings of vocation. What the Anabaptists wanted to do, explicitly and implicitly, was recapture the sense that being a Christian shaped—and even transformed—every aspect of life.[66]

Graber Miller goes on to list six core beliefs that reflect today's Mennonite sense of "radical sending"—of living one's faith in daily life. The three below capture the essence of that practice:

> 1. *Calling should be understood primarily and fundamentally as being a follower of Jesus Christ.* When asked about his vocation, an early Anabaptist reportedly said, "My vocation is to follow Christ. To make a living I am a tailor."[67] . . .
>
> Such a calling to discipleship is not just about professions and paid work, but shapes how Mennonite Christians engage in relationships, how they spend their free time, how they form and keep and relate to families, whether or not they choose to have children, how they parent, how they make decisions about money, how they open themselves to others who are different, and how they serve others. . . .[68]
>
> 2. *A Christian theology of vocation in Mennonite perspective honors and blesses the ways followers of Jesus live out their faith in their occupational, professional, and worldly roles.* Mennonites need to keep working out the relationship between what they do *in church* and what they do *as church* in their lives. "Being the church" includes being scattered into various places of employment within society's institutions. These locations will likely include not only teaching, health care and social services but also professional engagement in political and economic life. The church can be the church in various voluntary organizations working to change society, in justice-conscious businesses,

in creative work of many types, and even in public office when one's work is geared toward serving God and the common good, "Being church" ought to penetrate these work-a-day worlds. . . .

Christians are called not just to be Christians "in general," but to be Christians in concrete locations—as friends, as spouses, as parents, as citizens, and as laborers and professionals. Christians express their faith in and often through organizational and institutional and relational structures, including at the places where they work. As such, the church should bless those who serve the cause of Christ in their various, flexible, ever-changing "stations" in life.[69]

In a footnote for this last passage, Graber Miller adds:

In his article titled "God's Double Agents" *The Mennonite* (19 April 2005), 9–10, Wally Kroeker suggested commissioning people for their day-to-day work, planning a series of "workplace testimonies" for churches, having pastors visit members at their work settings, or having people attend a special Sunday service in their work garb.

Graber Miller continues his list of core practices:

5. *God's callings may not always line up with our initial hopes, expectations or particular occupational preparation. . . .* Sometimes [our being compelled to do work that offers no passion or joy] is referred to as "making a living," but Mennonites and other Christians ought to seek for themselves and for others humane systems and workplaces where all can not only "make a living," but "make a life." That is to say, lives that are integrated, where work flows out of who we are and allows us to express our faith through relationships, our interactions with friends and strangers, an attentiveness to the creative products of our labor, and the use of our natural and schooled gifts and abilities.[70]

"Minister" Means Every Believer

This Anabaptist theology of vocation is a key understanding among Mennonites in leadership, as well as the rank and file. Ryan Ahlgrim, a Richmond, Virginia, Mennonite leader, expresses it this way:

It is common in Mennonite churches for the word "minister" to refer to every believer. We are all called to serve one another and the world. . . . Mennonites frequently refer to 1 Corinthians 12 about the nature of the Body of Christ (all have their necessary roles and dignity) and Ephesians 4:11–12 (leaders are for "equipping the saints for the work of ministry"). . . . The point is to get everyone into the church's ministry, doing a ministry.

The rituals of the church are "just symbols" (which, in theory, aren't needed at all). On the positive side, this approach denies that there is a line between the sacred and the profane. Rather than making all of reality profane, I think this approach more rightly makes all reality sacred. For believers, every meal is a Eucharist. Every bath a baptism.[71]

. . . In Mennonite churches there is a much-reduced distinction between "clergy" and "laity." We don't even use these terms. Instead we sometimes refer to "credentialed leaders," "elders" (un-credentialed and usually term-limited leaders), and "members" (which includes everybody). And although credentialed leaders (clergy) typically preside at the congregation's rituals, actually any member affirmed by the congregation may baptize, serve communion, or preach. Spiritual authority resides in the congregation as a whole, not in particular persons. The congregation together discerns the will of God for the life of the church.

This, I think, affects how we view our workaday lives and vocations. The church fosters a sense of each of us being equipped for spiritual discernment and Christian practice, and so we bring the ethical and missional/service dimensions of our faith into our vocations. All of us are ministers in every aspect of life—at church, at home, in the workplace, and in social activities.[72]

Another Mennonite leader, author John D. Roth, offers comments on how Mennonites understand their witness in the world:

The key question of church growth . . . is less a matter of Christian doctrine than it is of Christian practice—formative practices shaped by a worshipping community that spill out of the congregation to find expression in the ordinary flow of daily life. . . .

Sunday morning spills out beyond the confines of the church into the more routine, public world of our everyday life.[73]

Roth opens his next chapter with a quote from American theologian Bryan Stone: "What the Gospel needs most is not intellectual brokers or cultural diplomats, but rather saints who have taken up the way of the cross and in whose lives the gospel is visible, palpable, and true."[74] Roth goes on to add, "Sermons provide a bridge between the text of Scripture and the context of daily life."[75]

Pointing to a transformational understanding of Christ's presence, Roth concludes:

In baptism and communion Christ assured his followers that he would be present with them. Although Christians have stretched their vocabulary to describe the exact nature of Christ's presence in these ceremonies, the promise of Christ's presence is nonetheless as real today as it was two thousand years ago. Perhaps the biggest challenge for believers is not formulating precise theological language; it is praying for the gift of grace to recognize Christ's presence in the humble realities of everyday life.[76]

Testimony from a Registered Nurse

That understanding is not lost on Patricia Rohrer, a registered nurse and a Mennonite living in Richmond, Virginia. She finds that her faith connects directly to her daily life as she reflects on her personal vocation as ministry:

> *I am not an ethnic Mennonite. I was baptized, raised, and educated as a Roman Catholic from which a belief and value system was instilled. My faith journey took a turn when I met my husband-to-be while I was in nursing school. There were approximately one hundred conscientious objectors staffing the hospital where I was training. This group of young men was impressive in their obvious solidly lived values and faith-based commitment to service. Marrying into the Mennonite faith nurtured a new Christian perspective of lived beliefs.*
>
> *I worked as a staff nurse in a hospital for numerous years, but it was not until I took a position teaching practical nursing students that I fully realized how a vocation could also be a ministry. I still remember talking with another faculty person in my first year of teaching about how our job was truly a mission. My reflections throughout my career as a nurse educator seem to emphasize service, community, and reconciliation.*
>
> *I had been personally and vocationally sheltered and unprepared for the diversity of background experiences, abuse, single parenting, family dynamics, and emotional and psychological issues some students brought with them to class and clinical. However, all students had the same goal: to become nurses to help them rise above their current situation in order to provide a stable and safe environment for themselves, their children, or family. This became my service to them: to counsel, listen, support, encourage, believe in them, remediate, and advocate. This became as much a part of my role as was teaching nursing. Trust and confidentiality were foundational in establishing and modeling healthy relationships. This was (is) not a conscious decisive act by me, but rather an unconscious extension in my work environment, of my personal integrated faith-based beliefs and values.*
>
> *Low self-esteem was a common thread with many students. Through our nine months as a "community/family of learners" students learn how to work together as a team, make solid and critical decisions, help and support each other, address each other's needs, and guide each other. Inevitably, self-esteem improved with a sense of personal accomplishment*

that some had previously rarely experienced. A community of learners with a common goal provides many students with a welcomed stability and opportunities to grow personally and professionally.

Along with service and community, reconciliation is another Mennonite belief that I have attempted to embrace in the workplace. I have had a number of opportunities to model or facilitate love, forgiveness, and conflict resolution among students. Learning how to resolve personal issues with peers is a task not easily accomplished. Modeling and teaching nonjudgmental attitudes and soft skills occur on a daily basis. All these are crucial in the healthcare environment as well as in one's personal life.

Over the years, I have offered up in prayer some of my students' personal issues during Sunday worship while also reenergizing myself through prayer or sermons in preparation for the week ahead.

Evangelism is not necessarily a part of how I share my faith, but rather I attempt to share an honest and authentic self. Students have acknowledged this verbally and in notes to me. Most recently I received a random note of "special thanks" from a student who wrote, " . . . Thanks for all your help, you are always willing to help and to encourage me along the way. Thanks again for believing in me. . . . Keep me in your prayers." Verbally she told me it was evident I was a Christian. I am humbled in the Lord for having the opportunity to work in a vocation I love and integrate who I am in the workplace.[77]

Our Roman Catholic Connection

As Pope Francis, elected pope in 2013, has focused his energies on dealing with "ecclesiastical narcissism,"[78] he has increasingly targeted clericalism as a fundamental illness of the church. Writing about the pope's "reform of the laity," Roger Landry reported that in 2011, prior to being elected pope, then-Cardinal Jorge Mario Bergoglio lamented:

> We priests tend to clericalize the laity. We do not realize it, but it is as if we infect them with our own disease. And the laity—not all, but many—ask us on their knees to clericalize them, because it is more comfortable to be an altar server than the protagonist of a lay path. We cannot fall into that trap—it is a sinful complicity.[79]

In that same interview with an Argentinian news agency, the future pope added:

> The layperson is a layperson and has to live as a layperson with the power of baptism, which enables him to be a leaven of the love of

God in society itself, to create and sow hope, to proclaim the faith, not from a pulpit but from his everyday life. And, like all of us, the layperson is called to carry his daily cross—the cross of the layperson, not of the priest.[80]

In *Evangelii Gaudium*, Pope Francis' apostolic exhortation released in November 2013, the same themes emerged:

102. Lay people are, put simply, the vast majority of the people of God. The minority—ordained ministers—are at their service. . . . Even if many are now involved in the lay ministries, this involvement is not reflected in a greater penetration of Christian values in the social, political and economic sectors. It often remains tied to tasks within the Church, without a real commitment to applying the Gospel to the transformation of society.[81]

A blogger, writing on a Roman Catholic activist site, summarized:

The lay vocation is not aimed at the inner life of the Church; it's aimed at transforming the secular world from within. . . .
We need a Copernican revolution in Church thinking, perhaps. Laity can bring their professional skills to the parish and chancery, yes. What's infinitely more important is that they bring their Christianity to their professions.[82]

A Roman Catholic priest, Anthony Shonis, served most of his priesthood as a teacher. He found himself, at the age of fifty-five, appointed pastor of a church. In order to know his parishioners better, "I began an activity that proved so fruitful that I have continued it for nine years. I began visiting parishioners at their workplace."[83] After briefly relating the process for his visits, Shonis comments:

For me this is the beginning of the Sunday/Monday connection . . . This is where the rubber meets the road, where people really do carry out the dismissal rite (actually a commission rite) to spread the Gospel. . . . Practicing the spirituality of work, and helping people understand that work is not simply an economic activity but rather a way for us to cooperate in God's plan for a better world, is exactly what Pope John Paul II had in mind when he talked about a new evangelization.

In his comment on the Dismissal rite, Shonis refers to the book *The Mass Is Never Ended*, by Gregory F. Augustine Pierce. Pierce, a layman and well-known Roman Catholic author, argues that the Dismissal—the "sending" at the end of worship— "should be the culmination of all that has happened before it . . . [that is to say,] the most important part of the Mass."[84]

Pierce believes that

> work—at least all *good* work—includes all the activity we do to help make the world a better place, a place more like the way God would have things, what Jesus of Nazareth called the *kingdom* or the *reign* of God. . . .
>
> Wouldn't it be great if those of us who believed in this mission could get together once a week (or even more often, occasionally) to remind ourselves of our mission, to reflect on how we are doing to thank and ask God for forgiveness and help, to be strengthened and trained and motivated to go back out and give it another try? Even better, wouldn't it be great if our church could design a liturgy that would accomplish all this?[85]

Pierce contends that the Roman Catholic Mass is that liturgy, which culminates in a "sending forth" of the congregation into the world, to carry out the mission of Jesus in proclaiming the kingdom of God. From the viewpoint that the sending forth is the focal point of the Mass and the beginning of our service—in the world—then each week, when the congregation gathers, the Mass provides opportunities for:

- *Coming Back*—Returning from the mission fields where we have been serving and gathering with others who have been on similar journeys; making the confession that we've fallen short in proclaiming the kingdom; and being forgiven, so we're ready to go out again;

- *Preparing to Be Sent Forth Again*—By listening to Scripture and sermon that open our ears to the Word of God; by proclaiming through the creed that "we are all on the same page"; by praying for the church and for the world, and especially that we might be equipped for God's mission;

- *Transubstantiating Our Gifts*—Offering money, bread, and wine—imperfect fruits of our labor—to be transformed; and praying the prayer Jesus taught us, to be reminded of our true mission;

- *Food for the Journey*—Receiving holy food that we may become the body of Christ for the world; and, duly commissioned, being sent forth once again to proclaim the kingdom.

William Droel, for many years the editor of the National Center for the Laity's *Initiatives*, is quoted on the back cover of Pierce's book: "There is only one Mass. . . . It is our work, Monday through Saturday. It is our worship on Sunday. Greg Pierce urges us to live the Mass all-at-once." And Pierce himself concludes with, "Leave the church [after Mass] as if you had been shot out of a cannon, embrace your mission to make this a better world, and develop your own spirituality of work to sustain you."[86]

Lutherans "equipping congregations," Mennonites "being church," and Roman Catholics being commissioned by the Dismissal. Each provides us with practical ways that congregations can become radically sending communities focused on "equipping the saints" for their ministry.

GOING FORTH

1. *For noticing or sharing with others:* What idea or thought in this chapter caught your imagination, surprised you, challenged your assumptions, inspired you, raised a question, gave you hope, cautioned you, or opened a new perspective? How does that insight relate to your life as a sent Christian?

2. *For analysis:* Choosing two or three of the ideas that were described in this chapter, what might a congregation's life look like if it implemented those ideas?

3. *For reflection:* In light of the faith and daily life connections that these faith communities envision, what connections can you make with your own faith community?

4. *For discussion or discernment:* How might different denominations or congregations collaborate in supporting Christians in their daily lives?

5. *For action:* Engage someone who belongs to another faith tradition (Christian or not) in a conversation about the connection between faith and daily life or work. What did you learn?

Sending Congregations

We are all called to God's table as beloved
members of the Body of Christ—this is the great
privilege of our faith; the great responsibility
of our faith is to carry that love into the world.

OFFERTORY SENTENCE, TRINITY EPISCOPAL CHURCH,
MILFORD, MASSACHUSETTS

Becoming a "sending congregation"—to live into the base-camp model offered in the first chapter—requires a number of shifts in thinking (see the chapter on "Shifts in Perspective" on page 109) and a willingness to learn strategies for overcoming institutional obstacles enshrined in tradition (see the chapter on "Roadblocks to Radical Sending" on page 96). In spite of those challenges, there are congregations which have begun to equip their members not only to comprehend the Sunday-Monday connection, but to live and embrace it.

Authors Paul Sparks, Tim Soerens, and Dwight J. Friesen describe their journeys in leading and mentoring several such congregations in their book *The New Parish: How Neighborhood Churches Are Transforming Mission, Discipleship and Community*. Sparks's determination to connect his congregation with daily life realities arose from a six-month sabbatical hiking the Pacific Northwest. On his sixteen-hundred-mile trek,

> he would walk for four days and then stop in a particular place to explore church ministries and neighborhoods the other three days of the week. . . . Everywhere he walked, Paul discovered that when followers

of Jesus were sharing life together and living in the midst of the everyday realities of a particular place, there was a vibrancy and growing maturity to their faith.[87]

The other two authors—Friesen in academia and Soerens in his missional church experiments—were observing similar movements of the Holy Spirit. The three originally met for support and peer guidance, and their collaboration gave birth to the Parish Collective, now a network linking more than two hundred congregations and community organizations. Through their book, along with the Parish Collective and the annual Inhabit Conference, they seek to inspire reflection—and action—around the question, "What if God is up to something really big and global but it can only be discovered through the small and local?"[88] Their response to issues of church renewal and of daunting global problems is, essentially, "practicing the way of Jesus in place."[89]

The authors of *The New Parish* advocate that congregations reestablish their rootedness in their neighborhoods by reclaiming the ancient concept of "parish," the geographical area traditionally served by a local church and pastor. As Loren Mead describes it, "Parish means turf. Place. It includes within it a sense of the responsibility of the church for the people of the neighborhood, regardless of their relationship to the faith. . . . [It] also assumes close linkage to other parishes in a network of relationship."[90] *The New Parish* authors warn that after years of being immersed in commuter/consumer/web-based culture, "whole populations can develop a cocooned way of life." Calling Christian communities to become increasingly relational and place-rooted, they add:

> Being in collaborative relationships in real life (where you live, work, and play) awakens you to the effects of your actions both on people and on the place itself. It creates a context where your church can see whether its faith is more than just talk. The local place becomes the testing ground, revealing whether you have learned to love each other and the larger community around you. In essence, the parish is a dare to your faith.[91]

The authors acknowledge that such a shift in perspective will require work, not only from individuals in congregations but also from leaders accustomed to assessing progress by increasingly outdated measures, such as Sunday attendance, average pledge, and other benchmarks.

What is critical for receptivity to the new endeavor is the capacity to see how the Spirit may be at work in both the institutional church and the world at large. . . .

Learning to see the immeasurable and radical forces at play will require a new lens. It will require a new imagination that expands beyond our current concept of church and begins to track new patterns of renewal at work in the world. Ultimately, learning to see will require reorientation, new postures and new ways of practicing faith.[92]

Their insistence that congregations grow their definition of "being church" emerges out of a conviction that Christians are called by God to "to join in God's world-renewing project."[93]

God is up to something in neighborhoods, on the ground in real places. The church, in all its diversity, needs to figure out how to join in. We think God is putting forth a dare that, if practiced, could both revitalize church traditions, and develop a growing unity among members of various denominational expressions in the parish. More than that, it could help the church learn to give itself in love to the world around it.[94]

The congregation is a focal point both for engaging that work and for encouraging a relationship-centered self-understanding, reminding each person "that you are a loved child of God, that you are a full member of the body of Christ and that your primary vocation is full partnership in God's family business of reconciliation and renewal."[95] This intersection of community, formation, and mission—what the authors term "the life of holistic worship or 'faithful presence'"[96]—equips the congregation to live a fully contextualized life, participating in and engaging with the life of the entire community. The authors make the audacious claim, "Your Christ-like transformation is linked to the people in the place where you are."[97]

The daily life of each individual gives expression to that transformation:

Just as Christ "became flesh and blood, and moved into the neighborhood" (John 1:14, *The Message*), so also the people that comprise the local church in the parish are meant to be a tangible expression of God's love in the everyday reality of life.[98]

Such a life calls for support from a congregation that understands itself as a base camp, a "sending congregation," or as the Lutherans might call it, an "equipping community."

Developing a Sending Culture

As congregations become dissatisfied with living the twentieth-century model of institutional church, there are many different conceptions of how to celebrate the ministry of all the baptized and how to become more deeply rooted in the larger community. In The Episcopal Church, bishops and diocesan staffs responded generously when we asked them to name congregations they believed were modeling a "sending" culture. They pointed us toward congregations that were raising awareness of the Sunday-Monday connection—equipping the baptized for their daily life ministries, discovering creative approaches for deepening connections between their congregations and the surrounding neighborhood, opening their doors to "the other," developing ministries shared across lay/clergy and member/nonmember boundaries, and, over time, fostering a radically reshaped "sending" culture.

Becoming Outward-Facing

Becoming a base camp congregation is a community process that gradually shifts the focus of the congregation from "inside matters" and church-sponsored outreach to the world of their members' daily lives: family, work, community, school. Many congregations start with helping individual members recognize God's calling where they "live and move and have their being." Others initiate connections with their immediate, surrounding community. Successful efforts grow out of the congregation's culture and environment, and are shaped by listening to the voices in the faith community:

- Cara Spaccarelli, rector of *Christ Episcopal Church on Capitol Hill* (Diocese of Washington), wrote of her workplace visits to some twenty-five members of her congregation. She explained:

  I sent them three questions ahead of time:
  (1) Has your faith ever affected how you did your job?
  (2) What is the blessing of your work? What is the challenge? and
  (3) How does what happens on Sunday prepare you for your workweek?

  It was an amazing experience for me to have insight into where the majority of my parishioners spend the majority of their week. Pastorally, I have much greater understanding of this quadrant of their lives. Many had never thought of the questions I asked, but by the time I got there, they had answers—which I think was helpful for them (and me.) I then preached my Pentecost [2014] sermon, weaving together some anecdotes and insights from the experience.[99]

Spaccarelli added that the experience, and our inquiries, helped spark her imagination about how her congregation might become more intentional in supporting people in their work life ministry.

- At *St. Gabriel's in Douglasville, Pennsylvania* (Diocese of Bethlehem), the congregation's year-round approach to stewardship means that the rector and other church leaders send notes and cards reminding those in the congregation "that their daily work is an important part of their ministry, and thanking them for being the hands and feet of Jesus in their homes and workplaces," as rector David Robert Green described it. The parish motto, "Learning and Doing the Work of Jesus," points to discipleship and apostleship, with training and support offered in both areas. As Green wrote, "St. Gabriel's partners and members are encouraged to understand and be intentional about experiencing their mission and ministry in concentric circles out, from home to their neighborhood to their town to their diocese and to the ends of the earth."

  Worship consistently "includes reminders that all the baptized are empowered, authorized ministers and missionaries of the Good News of God's love in Christ." During services each week, those in the congregation share "God-incidences" and "God-moments" from the week before.

  The vestry's ESP (Expanding St. Gabe's Programs) working group is developing a "Neighborhood Network Ministry." Geographically defined neighborhood groups will be organized, designed to facilitate communication, pastoral care, and disaster preparedness as well as convene neighborhood fellowship gatherings, book studies, and other cell groups. "The early church grew person to person, neighborhood to neighborhood, so this concept is also a great evangelization strategy for reaching unchurched and underchurched folks in our post-Christian culture,"[100] added Green.

- In *Bartlesville* (Diocese of Oklahoma), the rector at *St. Luke's*, Lee Stephens, is "accused of having as my ministry mantra, 'I want every member to have at least one ministry inside the church and one ministry beyond the church'—and this is in addition to their vocational calling." Worship "has the regular 'gathering' and 'going' dynamics," and includes opportunities for lay members to preach. The vestry selects a member of the congregation each month for recognition as "our Prism of Christ and Christ's Ministry. This is not an award—simply a way to highlight and thank people for who they are and what they do. We lift [them] up as a model for others."[101]

- *St. John's, Oakland* (Diocese of California), is the congregation that originated the now-well-known confirmation program "Confirm, Not Conform." True to that heritage, rector Scott Denman reports:

  We are very involved in community organizing. For us, it's not about affirmation but invitation to action in the broader community. Teachers are involved in our education policy efforts. Those in environmental fields help lead efforts to change policy that will help lower the carbon footprint, etc.

  Quite frankly, we also confront clericalism. Laypeople read the gospel and we affirm the priesthood of all believers. Confirmands receive stoles that are signed by all the members of the congregation and they are placed around their necks at the confirmation celebration. Some of those students still have them as a reminder that they too have an important ministry.[102]

  The congregation has run a Lenten series focused on "how people bring their faith into their careers," and has shared the series with other congregations as well. Denman reports that dozens of congregation members have been sent to week-long community organizing leadership training and adds, "We are committed to an empowerment model, not a top down model."

Celebrating Stories

Two of the responding congregations offered stories drawn from their life together as a way of explaining their efforts to support and encourage the daily life ministry that all the baptized are called to exercise.

- Stephen Cuff, rector at *All Saints, Portsmouth* (Diocese of Southern Ohio), offered a picture of a congregation that intentionally "celebrates and affirms 'daily life ministry,' also known as baptismal ministry."

I'd like to write that there are liturgical practices and formational programs that foster this attitude, but alas, there are none. It seems to be more of an incarnational aspect of our life of faith in a comparatively small community (city has a population of 20,000 in a county of 75,000).

Portsmouth is a community where people know one another and are known. We're good at naming one another's gifts and calling those gifts into service for Christ and the Church. A parishioner is a morning DJ on the local radio station (in addition to serving as a lector on Sunday). Chip knows he has a voice in the community and a vehicle for sharing news. Tim and Stan own a home-cooking restaurant (in addition to serving on the altar guild and as Eucharistic ministers). They know how to feed a crowd: They do so for church dinners and are always offering their skills and resources for community endeavors. Kevin is a parishioner and a city councilman. He and I have a deal: He deals with politics in the city and I do so in the church. Barbara is a parishioner and a county librarian whose faith inspires her to foster wellness and literacy in a rural county in Kentucky. (She also leads our formation programs for children.)

Pastorally, I support daily life ministries by showing up. Expressing interest in and appearing where parishioners work (as appropriate) affirms vocation and helps me understand the joys and challenges that are part of any daily life ministry.

Perhaps it is an aspect of our Appalachian culture, perhaps it's just part of faith and life integrated in a small town—I admit to being surprised that our experience is not the norm across the church. The life of All Saints' Church would be greatly diminished if the tapestry of life and ministry in community were torn apart.[103]

- *St. Luke's, Bethesda, Maryland* (Diocese of Washington), offers a similarly diverse collection of stories about the daily life ministries that the congregation recognizes and celebrates. Rector Stephanie Nagley describes them as "stories of people being Christ in the world":

Kristin looks after her children, leads the children of the church in song, and runs *GoodSpeaks*, which connects issues in the news to actions and media from causes, nonprofits, and NGOs.

Jeff has looked out for the earth working for the environmental arm of the Department of Justice. He was there to litigate the British Petroleum disaster in the Gulf.

Connie travels the world for the sake of education for the State Department, and Betsy just recently retired from a program that brought young people together from all over the world.

Clay and Treva, now retired, quietly gather meals together each Friday for a men's shelter.

Jack gives uncounted hours to legal matters . . . for those who just need help.

Ched heads up the board for a mental health agency that St. Luke's began in the 1970s.

Marta leads yoga sessions at the free medical clinic after she finishes her work at the Department of Environmental Protection Agency.

Bob, a former ambassador, speaks to the church about the troubles in the Middle East and heads a nonprofit dedicated to helping people throughout the world live with dignity and respect.

Elliott serves Native Americans by providing legal counsel.

Dawn, a lawyer, makes T-shirts for a display about gun violence.

The liturgy and sermons make connection with everyday life, and prayers of the people are written each week "to include what is happening in our world right now and often what is happening in people's lives." Special liturgies are crafted for life passages. The offertory sentences and invitation demonstrate radical inclusion and hospitality:

We are now going to Holy Communion to receive the bread and wine. We place no restrictions upon it, for this is God's meal. So wherever you have come from, wherever you are going, whatever you believe or don't believe, come. For as we gather together with all our diversity and difference, we leave as one people, as people united to serve Christ in the world. Walk in love as Christ loved us and for the sake of love gave everything.

That theme continues, emphasizing "Jesus lived for us as [much as] he died for us," as the rector notes.

In describing what the congregation offers to support and train people for their daily life ministries, Nagley explains:

We offer a community where people can share their lives, their good days and bad days with each other and find support. Most of our Christian formation for adults is intended to help people reflect theologically and to deepen their awareness of who they are and to whom they are called. We also invite parishioners to come and share with each other their ministries. For example, one parishioner has an online site that connects people to various causes. She spoke to a church group about her work and why she does it. Another parishioner shared in that group her music ministry. Another his work in counterterrorism and another her understanding of immigration issues and women's issues.[104]

Shaping the Base Camp

Three congregations offered details of their intentional work to raise awareness of baptism as a commissioning to ministry and, beyond that, to create a base camp culture that shapes the congregation's life. That culture, in turn, equips individuals to live as "tangible expression[s] of God's love in the everyday reality of life,"[105] as *The New Parish* authors have expressed it.

- *Trinity Church in Milford, Massachusetts* (Diocese of Western Massachusetts), has intentionally engaged parishioners in exploring the seven different mission fields of daily life (home, work, community, wider world, leisure, spiritual health, and church), as taught by Member Mission Network.[106] Member Mission founder Wayne Schwab has led two training sessions at Trinity, with many of the leaders participating. Those trainings offer tools to help congregation members become intentional ambassadors for Christ in their various mission fields, as well as raising the congregation's awareness about supporting those daily life missions.[107] Rector Mac (William MacDonald) Murray adds:

We regularly have participants in small group studies (like book groups), national events (like the climate change march in New York City), local politics (gambling casino issues in Massachusetts are particularly hot right now), spiritual enhancement (something we call simple supper, Bible study, and prayer), and we have a very active social justice ministry here at Trinity—our youth groups are very involved with the Scattered Site Homeless Shelter families in our community and we have a large volunteer pool providing meals to members of our community who live in rooming houses (with no kitchen facilities).

Formation, advocacy, and social justice activities can all lay important foundations for a congregation's base camp ministry.

Murray describes additional formation activities for the congregation, in addition to the targeted training around ministry in daily life:

Our annual Lenten program focuses on the five questions in the baptismal covenant and we examine how we live into our responses to these questions. I also do regular baptism preparation classes which follow a similar format and delve into practical ways to live into "I will, with God's help." Our Stephen Ministry[108] program also has a number of trained Stephen Ministers who work with people to both get a handle on and further explore their daily life ministries.

Affirming members' daily work is an integral part of Murray's interactions with his congregants. As he explains, "I visit with parishioners and learn about their work and we talk about the ways their work is a witness (or not) to the Gospel (Good News of Jesus Christ)." In Sunday worship,

sermons generally include discussion about Member Mission (what is God calling you to in your life—work, play, community, church, family, etc.) as well as a clear sending out message at the offertory: We are all called to God's table as beloved members of the body of Christ. This is the great privilege of our faith; the great responsibility of our faith is to carry that love in to the world.[109]

- Lee Anne Reat, vicar of *St. John's in Columbus, Ohio* (Diocese of Southern Ohio), describes some of the complex challenges her mission church is embracing among the poor and the homeless in "the predominantly Appalachian inner-city neighborhood of Franklinton, also known as the 'Bottoms' because of its location in the flood plain at the confluence of two rivers and because of its poverty and general decay."[110] Much of the population struggles with deficits in educational, social, and financial dimensions, with inadequate housing, and with health issues including alcoholism, drug addiction, and obesity. Reat adds:

St. John's sits right in the middle of the community and has been a center of community activity for over one hundred years. Our ministries reflect our involvement in the neighborhood. . . .

On Sundays at 1:00 our second Eucharist of the day ["Street Church"] is held on a vacant lot at a busy intersection about one mile from the church building. This segment of our congregation is made up of homeless and marginally housed individuals and families, and people from other parts of the city who have joined our community over the years. . . .

Every Wednesday night (September–June) we welcome the community for worship, a children's choir, and dinner. Dinner is prepared by members of other congregations throughout Columbus. About 100 to 150 people attend weekly. During that time we open food and "stuff" pantries (blankets, coats, toiletries, etc.) and make appointments for counseling through the Ohio Benefit Bank, an online program linking people to needed community resources and benefit programs. Volunteer counselors meet with individuals to take them through the process.

The congregation includes members of several intentional communities engaging in community service and spiritual discernment. Reat details the values that define St. John's culture:

Our core value for ministry is that we do not have "outreach ministries." Everything we do reaches into our hearts through Christ and flows out to meet people where they are. Whether it's sending a birthday card to another member of the congregation or attending a rally at the Statehouse on a justice issue or assisting someone to find housing or coming together to worship, it's what we do as the body of Christ. . . .

Relationship, relationship, relationship. Whatever we do in ministry and whatever our members do in daily living is based, not on some result, but on the relationships built and maintained. We frequently hear, usually when we're at Street Church in a driving snow or rainstorm, "We know you'll always be here, no matter what." That assessment is based on years of experience by long-term residents of other church groups showing up for a while, then disappearing when it becomes too difficult or inconvenient. We're in the community to stay and the people know and trust us.

Reat goes on to mention the "sending" and "justice-oriented" practices of the congregation's liturgy, where "nourished by Word and Sacrament, [we] are sent out to love and serve Christ in one another." She adds:

One example of a specific liturgical practice at St. John's is our annual Stations of the Cross through the community on Good Friday. Each year we choose sites of pain and promise in the neighborhood and pray the stations there. In addition to prayers, we offer a short history of each site and mention ways to become involved in the organization represented or the issue brought forth.

Affirmation of parishioners' daily work is integral in the relational character of St. John's ministry in the community. The congregation's parish nurse, its focus on stabilizing families in need, and its deacons' work in Kairos prison ministry and in a human trafficking ministry all "serve as icons for service to the larger community."

Reat asked a group from the congregation, "Are we practicing 'radical sending' if our ministries are focused primarily on the neighborhood surrounding St. John's?" She reports:

The consensus was "yes." One woman who lives comfortably in the suburbs said, "If I went to another church, I might come down once or twice a year to serve dinner or write a check at Christmas, but I wouldn't know the people I now know whose lives are so different from mine and I wouldn't be able to call them my friends." Others commented that they read the paper or listen to the news through a different, more justice oriented lenses, that they are much more likely to engage a stranger in conversation rather than reacting in fear, and that their prayer lives have expanded far beyond themselves to others, and that those prayers express thanksgiving, not just petition, for the homeless friends they have made.[111]

- The people of *Robert E. Lee Memorial in Lexington, Virginia* (Diocese of Southwestern Virginia), have begun a small group designed to make the baptismal vows "a meaningful and powerful response to Christ carrying out his mission through us in every area of our lives," writes Peyton Craighill, a retired Episcopal priest and a member at Robert E. Lee.[112] Group members, including rector Tom Crittendon, join together in reflection on the promises of the Baptismal Covenant and how those promises relate to their daily life ministries. Craighill terms their weekly meeting "a spiritual power plant for the rest of our week."[113]

The group, which is being trained in using a coaching approach to leadership, hopes to spread their process to the rest of their congregation. In coaching, members "utilize active, reflective listening without judging, in a spirit of Christian love," and then work with the "coach-ee" to "come up with a 'declaration' that focuses on a goal or way the person envisions Christ working his mission in various aspects of life for a designated period of time—a week, a month, three months, a year."[114] In the group's discussion, each person brings life experiences, concerns, or discoveries that relate to that "declaration."

Their work with group members in helping formulate declarations is shaped by questions. Craighill shares an example:

In reflecting about your physics lab job at [the university], here are a number of questions about living out your five baptismal promises in daily life in this area of your mission-in-Christ:

1. *The apostles' teaching; communion; fellowship; prayer life*
   How can you be intentionally aware of Christ-in-mission in your lab?
   And how he invites you to share with him in his mission?
   In connection with your lab experience:
   How much do you reflect on relevant Bible passages?
   How do you relate your Sunday Eucharist to your Monday-through-Friday experiences?
   How do you share koinonia in your lab?

2. *Resisting evil; repentance; turning to the Lord*
   (I call this promise my heavenly GPS system. In following the Lord when I lose my way, it gets me back on track.)
   When you feel out of sync with Christ working through you to advance his mission, how do you ask him to get you on track again with him? What does repentance mean in this context?

3. *Proclaiming Good News of God in Christ by word and by example*
   How do you share Christ's Good News both indirectly and directly in your lab?

4. *Seek and serve Christ in all persons, loving your neighbor as yourself*
   How do you share Christ's love for all people in your lab?

5. *Strive for justice and peace, respect the dignity of all humans*
   How do you respect the dignity (worth) of all the people in your lab?

Reinventing Church Structure

Colchester Federated Church (CFC) in Colchester, Connecticut, offers a singular example of a congregation so focused on supporting the ministries of laypeople in the world that it rethought and reframed its entire organizational structure. As documented in *The Empowering Church*, pastor Davida Foy Crabtree and the members of the CFC congregation reshaped the church's governance, programs, and property-usage. The group spent a number of years "designing a new organizational structure for the church which [would] give approximately equal weight to 'sending-them-out' as it does to 'holding-them-here,'"[115] requiring a systemic change in the church's understanding of mission. They reconceived the processes of becoming a member, of selecting leaders, of supporting spiritual and personal growth, and of evaluating programs.

Crabtree herself did not implement the changes in the church's structure that her book describes. That implementation was left to her successor, according to Pastor Linda Barnes.[116] The changes continue to bear fruit, particularly among the lay leaders, one of whom announced to Barnes on her arrival in 2006, "We are an empowered laity." Barnes remarked, "This church takes more seriously than any church I've known their responsibility to the community." Noting that ministry in daily life has been a lifelong emphasis of her ministry, Barnes added, "I view my role as an orchestra leader."

Crabtree's book itself makes no claim to offer a program to be adopted wholesale by other congregations. Instead, it makes the case for the importance of doing the hard work of relationship building and discernment in order to grow new visions for congregational life in indigenous soil. Crabtree's reflections on structure for mission; on the renewal of the church; on the theology of work; and on management, systems, and ministry make her book a thought-provoking read. It offers a case study of a wide-ranging and deep-rooted reconception of the role of the congregation as a support for the work of laity in the world.

"Sending Forth" More Than "Reaching Out"

Some of these congregations—like many, many others—have embraced congregation-based outreach ministries as a way to become more engaged with the surrounding community. Such ministries— feeding kitchens, clothing drives, and financial literacy education, for instance—are important congregationally centered expressions of Christ's compassion for God's people. Such work can often prepare the hearts of individuals to perceive what God is doing beyond the walls of the church, both in the world and in their daily lives. Once we see what God is up to, we're more often able to hear God's call.

What distinguishes "sending" congregations is their focus less on evangelism or on outreach activities by the congregation, and more on finding creative ways to support individual members in their daily, outside-of-church-context lives. For some, pastors have spent time with members in their places of work connecting Sunday with Monday.

For some, that support has taken the shape of discussion and learning groups that foster reflection by individuals on how they might "be Christ" in their daily life environment. For others, moving toward being a sending congregation has involved recognizing the presence of the "others" just outside their doors—the downtown workers, the tourists, the government officials, and the schoolchildren—in order to provide a ministry to and with them. For still others, that has meant lending the weight of liturgical recognition and celebration to the world of daily life—where members of the congregation spend the majority of their time—so that those participating in worship are sent out, strengthened and renewed to recognize and affirm God at work through them as they go about their day-to-day lives.

Such "sending congregations" give their people a variety of tools to go be the church.

Our next chapter offers first-person accounts from people who have discerned some of the ways that God has been working in their daily lives.

GOING FORTH

1. *For noticing or sharing with others:* What idea or thought in this chapter caught your imagination, surprised you, challenged your assumptions, inspired you, raised a question, gave you hope, cautioned you, or opened a new perspective? How does that insight relate to your life as a sent Christian?

2. *For analysis:* What characteristics do you see as important to enable a faith community to become a "sending congregation"?

3. *For reflection:* What do you find challenging about the work these congregations are doing? Why?

4. *For discussion or discernment:* What "small and local" practice(s) might you like to see adopted in your congregation that would support individual members in their daily lives? What difference might such practices make for your members?

5. *For action:* Imagine one way your congregation might recognize or celebrate the daily lives of your members, and talk to the appropriate leader(s) in your congregation about implementing your idea.

Servants
in Daily Life

How can asphalt be a spiritual experience?
How can forty-ton tractor-trailers be part of a godly life?
These are the questions that come up when I attempt
to find connections between my vocation and my spiritual
journey. Where is my God in all of this business?
How does my spiritual life mesh with my professional life?

THE MANAGER OF A PAVING COMPANY[117]

For a follower of Jesus, these questions are not unique to a paving contractor. Change the context to a baker, soccer mom or dad, a volunteer member of a community organization board, or a citizen getting ready to vote: How does my spiritual life mesh with my daily life?

During the Last Supper, along with the foot washing, the conversation among the disciples began to focus on who is the greatest. Jesus responds:

> The kings of the Gentiles lord it over them; and those in authority over them are called benefactors. But not so with you; rather the greatest among you must become like the youngest, and the leader like one who serves. For who is greater, the one who is at table or the one who serves? Is it not the one at table? But I am among you as one who serves. (Luke 22:25–27)

And, in summary, "The greatest among you will be your servant" (Matthew 23:11).

Be a servant? That's like being at another person's beck and call, someone's doormat, having to kowtow, to bow and scrape. Certainly that is not what Jesus is calling us to be.

No. Think again. Jesus's reference to being a servant is a reflection on his own life of being there for others, whether it's five thousand hungry people, a party where the wine has run out, a blind beggar being healed, a storm being calmed, or ultimately, his death and resurrection. He lived his life for others—all in the name of God.

The above paving contractor's questions are less about asphalt and forty-ton trucks than they are about how do I, following Jesus's example, serve those with whom I work, live, play, or meet. It is in serving that we reflect Jesus in our daily lives. How then does being a servant, for the Christian, get translated into daily life?

We will approach this through the eyes of a group of people from St. Paul's Episcopal Church, Richmond, Virginia, that meets monthly to discuss Christian values in the marketplace, using case studies from secular sources such as the *New York Times* and religious sources such as the Christian *High Calling*.[118] In one conversation they focused on the essential Christian values they want to carry from Sunday into Monday.

Humility

"As a Christian," one participant suggested, "humility is key. I realize I don't have all the answers, whether it is as a manager, parent, or community member. That allows me to be open to others and their gifts. This applies to personal as well as professional issues." Christian author Rick Warren put it this way, "It is not thinking less of yourself but thinking of yourself less."[119] Humility opens up the potential of the other while acknowledging our own limitations. Rather than a sign of weakness, it puts our own gifts in the perspective of those of others. It is vital to any aspect of life, be it family, business, community, or church. Humility is a condition, an attitude, a mindset of the Spirit. "Walk humbly with your God," the prophet Micah (6:8) advises—and with others, we might add.

Humility in action is like the car mechanic seeking advice from a fellow worker. It's the manager building a team. It's the board member recognizing his dependence on others to resolve a funding problem. It's the teacher being open to the ideas of the student and the student recognizing the validity of her fellow classmate. It's the parent seeking support with a family problem. It's Pope Francis's approach to where he lives, the car he drives, and the clothes he wears.

Another participant told this story of a friend who was the Roman Catholic bishop of Richmond. "He (the bishop) was approaching a parking lot soon to be transformed into an educational center commemorating the 1786 Virginia Statute for Religious Freedom authored by Madison, Jefferson, and Monroe. Arriving for the center's ground breaking, as he entered the lot, he went over to its two attendants, greeted each one of them, asked how they were doing and then thanked them for their service. In a similar way he proceeded to greet some of the dignitaries like the mayor and the member of the U.S. House of Representatives." Through this simple exchange, he lived out humility. High or low, rich or poor, this bishop affirms Christ's serving the people he meets as part of his Christian faith, and in the process, he empowers the other.

Empathy

Another St. Paul's participant chimed in with a different value from a more secular source—that of Stephen R. Covey, a motivational writer and speaker. Covey's mantra: "Seek first to understand, then to be understood,"[120] echoes a phrase in the prayer attributed to St. Francis: "Grant that we may not seek . . . to be understood as to understand." In a word, that is what empathy is—taking the other seriously, walking a mile in the other person's moccasins (as Native Americans might say), of being accessible and open, be it on the job, at home, or in the community. Another participant fleshed it out: listening to others, drawing out the other's talents, recognizing and empowering those around you, investing in those with whom you associate in daily life wherever that may be. As Christians we need to own this as our calling—this ministry of presence, of empathy.

Jesus underscores empathy: "Do to others as you would have them do to you" (Matt. 7:12), something we Christians know as the Golden Rule—a concept that joins us with every other major religion. Empathy is the action dimension of being a servant. How do I reach out to the other on the job, in the family, and in my community? What is it like to be present in the way the Samaritan was to the injured man on the side of the road? It is the manager making space for the co-worker/parent whose child is sick; it is the politician listening, intent on finding common ground with another whose views differ; it is the suburban woman gaining support from the homeless mother during the congregation's feeding program as they share their children's drug problems; it is the native-born worker sharing lunch with the newly hired foreign-born worker, not only welcoming her, but taking the time to identify with her issues of adjustment; it is as simple as welcoming the new neighbor and as intense as advocating for health care for the poor before the state government.

Again, Jesus: "You are the salt of the earth. . . . You are the light of the world" (Matt. 5:13–14). One of the St. Paul's group reflected:

> One statement from the (Episcopal) Baptismal Covenant has had special emphasis for me: "I will respect the dignity of every human being." It is a core value of my social work profession as well. To be effective in working with mandated clients, people from all walks of life, it helps to look for the human potential, each person's strengths and who they are, not just their problems or what they have done.

A Virginia Supreme Court justice put it this way:

> As I remain true to this charge (as a Supreme Court justice), though, I also cannot help but be informed and influenced by my faith. My faith is not a patina that rests lightly on what I do; rather it is an integral part of who I am. In this regard, my challenge is no different than that of each person reading these words. Is not an accountant, a newspaper reporter, or a stay-at-home mom also informed and influenced by their faith as they perform their daily tasks? Are we different than the fishermen, tax collectors, and centurions whom Jesus of Nazareth touched and transformed? I suggest that we are not, and that our faith ought to inform and influence our work in three primary ways: We are called to glorify God in all we do; to do justice and to love mercy; and to treat our colleagues, coworkers, clients, and customers as we wish to be treated.[121]

The paving contractor had his own thoughts:

> I am an agent for God's grace through the way I interact and am involved with all of my employees. The compassion that I feel and the concern that I communicate to all my people can be spiritual blessings for me as well as for them. . . . Moreover, the way I conduct myself can hopefully serve as an example of spiritual faithfulness. It is my hope that my behavior can reflect my Christian values.[122]

Servant Love

No discussion of values for the Christian in daily life would be complete without focusing on love. As we know, it comes up more often in the family, less in the community, and rarely in the workplace, except, "I love my job!" At the root of being a servant, though, is love. But love, in the English language, is a many splendored thing. We love chocolate, love basketball, love our parents, spouse, partner, or children—and love our job.

Servant love reaches beyond all of them. It is the Samaritan's love of the injured man left on the side of the road. It is Jesus's response to the questioning scribe: "Love your neighbor as yourself" (Mark 12:28–31). The letter-writer John points to the source: "God is love" (1 John 4:16). At its root, undergirding all that the Christian does as a servant—his humility, her empathy, their life—is that love which springs from God and radiates out as ripples in a pond. *Agape*, the Greeks called it: outgoing, unconditional, serving love, a love that is the nonjudgmental inclusive presence for the other.

Which leads to a key dimension of living the life of Christ as a servant: Know yourself as a beloved child of God. After all, Jesus did say, "Love your neighbor *as* yourself." Each of us is made in God's image (Genesis 1:27) and we are "fearfully and wonderfully made" (Psalm 139:14). To put it in the colloquial, "God don't make no junk!" At the core of one's servant sojourn with God is one's own sense of self-worth stemming from that *Christ love*, that love of self. It is that self-confidence that enables the servant to love the other, to be both humble and empathetic.

Prayer

Intimate, ongoing conversation with God is an essential value for practicing our faith in daily life. It can be a formal prayer from a prayer book or the more spontaneous, running, and unspoken: "Help me, Lord, with this," or "What do I say next, Lord?" which acknowledges one's ultimate dependence on God. It undergirds all that we are and do. For the Christian, being a servant in everyday living is an ongoing prayerful journey with Christ, up and down hills, sometimes with potholes and detours, but also with straight places and gardens. It is this inner journey with God that enables our external sojourn to be authentically servant.

Gratitude

All of which leads to gratitude, of being thankful for all that I am by God's grace. "Thanks be to God." Isn't thanksgiving more than a liturgical mantra? Doesn't that sum up what life in Christ, life in the marketplace, home, and community, is all about—a life lived in gratitude? And thanks be to God for the calling to be a servant.

Teresa of Ávila, a sixteenth-century Spaniard who toiled relentlessly to reform her several Carmelite convents, put it this way:

May today there be peace within.
May you trust God that you are exactly where you are meant to be.
May you not forget the infinite possibilities that are born of faith.
May you use those gifts that you have received,
and pass on the love that has been given to you.
May you be content knowing you are a child of God.
Let this presence settle into your bones,
and allow your soul the freedom to sing, dance, praise and love.
It is there for each and every one of us.[123]

Servants on the Journey

Putting these values—humility, empathy, love, prayer, gratitude—to work as daily practices is the challenge we face when we decide to go beyond being Sunday-only worshippers of Christ to being Jesus-followers in our everyday lives. Like the disciples that Jesus sent out to proclaim the Good News and bring healing wherever they went, present-day followers grow their own faith as they share their experiences.

What follow are stories, stories told by individual Christians who have discerned that calling and found their true identity in their work, home, and community. In their own words, these Christ-followers offer their transformational stories about learning to understand themselves as people sent out—radically sent—by God to make God's presence known in the world.

As noted earlier in my (Fletcher's) story in "Our Journey to Radical Sending," from the beginning of my ordained life, I have visited members of the congregations I have served in their places of work, including their homes. The conversations generally have begun with "What do you do here?" and flowed to "What is the Sunday-Monday, the faith connection with what you do here?" For at least 85 percent of those I have visited, this is the first time that question has been raised—yet that is the very place where Christians spend most of their God-given time and talent. Radical sending calls the Church to pay attention to that question: What is the Sunday-Monday, the faith connection, the Monday morning hangover from your Sunday morning experience with what you do here, be it on the job or in the community or at home?

Below are some real live stories of real live Christians who are works-in-progress in connecting Sunday with Monday—told in their own words. An additional story, from money manager Philip Brooks of Richmond, Virginia, can be found at www.RadicalSending.com.

A Lawyer's "Aha!"

I am a corporate "transactional" attorney, which means that I work for a corporation (UPS Freight), as opposed to a law firm, and that I primarily work on transactions that the company is involved in, such as buying or selling real estate or entering into a contract for some type of services or goods. Because of this I work with people in many different positions within the company. From service center managers that are at locations all over the country to senior management here in Richmond, I negotiate and write all kinds of contracts—contracts to buy software, to lease trucks, to acquire janitorial services, to hire guards at our terminals. If it involves a contract of any type, I'm usually involved in it. They can be very insignificant contracts or multimillion-dollar contracts.

When Fletcher Lowe originally asked if he could visit me at work to discuss the "faith connection," that is, the connection between what I do to make a living and my faith, I agreed reluctantly. Not because I was reluctant to talk with Fletcher or because I was reluctant to talk about either my work or my faith. I just wasn't sure I saw any connection between the two. So, I agreed, but planned to rely on Fletcher to steer the conversation, because I really couldn't draw a connection there. I mean, after all, how could working as an attorney for a trucking company tie in to God's work anyway?

In our discussion, he challenged me to see how the gifts I have and the work I do is in fact God's work. That drafting up a contract fairly is applying my faith and the values rooted in my faith. That treating my fellow employees with respect, behaving in an ethical manner, and being able to help two parties work through issues and come up with a problem-solving approach, rather than a conflict-based disagreement, is doing God's work. That, in fact, doing what I have the skills to do, using whatever talents I may have, is God's work.

It was a revelation to me! I tended (and still tend—it's hard to re-train my brain after forty-eight years) to view "God's work" as what the priests, choir directors, youth ministers, and Mother Teresas of the world do. I viewed the "work world" as separate from the "faith world." To my mind, God's work is things like tutoring at Woodville, serving guests at CARITAS, even writing a check to the Carpenter's Kids (out-reach programs of the congregation). It turned that assumption on its ear to see that maybe simply applying the talents God gave me is, in fact, also doing "God's work." As dry and unfaith-like as writing up a contract sounds—it did seem possible that somehow that type of work might also serve God's purpose. And, in that setting, St. Paul's and the community there isn't separate, but is a foundation, as Fletcher likes to say, a "base camp," for the rest of the week—a place to focus, resupply, and prepare to go back out and do whatever work is set out before me.

I suppose that is the bottom line—that God's work can take the shape of every type of labor and effort in the world. All that variety of work has to occur in order for the world to move forward; for the community of humankind to prosper (in a spiritual sense, as well as a material one). And the most important thing is to use what gifts we each have, gifts as diverse as the work to be done, to tackle the work that is set before us. What a concept. God is truly amazing!

Lisa McKnight, Richmond, Virginia[124]

A Trial Attorney Turned Restaurateur

When I was young, going to church was a paradoxical distraction from an unhappy home made so by parents that fought bitterly and openly. Learning from negative example, I've managed to do my part to have a wonderful marriage, a wife, and three great children I love dearly . . . with God's help of course.

Going to church after I married was de rigeur. After all, I married a PK (preacher's kid). I listened earnestly during worship, served in leadership, attended innumerable covered dish suppers, and so on. In hindsight I realize that I didn't tread too deeply into the spiritual waters of my faith when my children were young. After all, I was a busy, important trial attorney with only so much time to net-cast for things that weren't immediate to our corporate success as a family. Not to say that going to church, without digging deeper, lacked value. Quite the contrary.

A little more than ten years ago my idea of what it meant to be a Christian began to change when I learned about a new organization being sponsored by our church, St. Mark's Episcopal in San Antonio. It's called the Work+Shop, and is directed by, of all people, an attorney who hung up his lucrative law guns for seminary, ordination, and postgraduate work at Oxford in New Testament Studies, particularly the life, writings, and ministry of Paul. [At this organization] I met my career bungee-jumping friend, John Lewis, director of the Work+Shop.

I too was undergoing a career change when John and I met. I left the everyday practice of law to run a hospitality, food, and beverage business I purchased from a good friend and law client when he asked, "Are you tired of trying lawsuits yet?" In the intervening years I've participated in many different Work+Shop groups and activities. The one dearest to my heart is simply known as "The Tuesday Morning Reflection Group."

My shorthand description of Tuesday morning's group is reverse Bible study. Here's how it works: At seven o'clock in the morning, between five and twenty people gather in a comfortable meeting room in our diocesan offices. We come to order and center ourselves with a short prayer and collect for the day. A question is then asked: "Who has a story to tell?" Two or three usually emerge, and are followed by a minute or two of quiet reflection, and a request for Bible stories or scriptural references that would inform us of how Christ would have responded, or how his example would inform us to be in the particular situation. Sometimes the stories and reflection are validations that the reporter built on past work in the group and "got it right." Sometimes it is the opposite—a blown opportunity, a hasty answer that did harm. (I remember the first and second chapters of the Letter of James regarding "the tongue is a fire" in such instances.)

Years in this group have shaped me, and my fellow Tuesday morning goers, into being better people . . . more intentional Christians . . . more often like Christ . . . more capable agents for bringing the kingdom into human interactions. Daily dilemmas now faze me much less, as I am a quieter, more deliberative person (with a long way to go). "Proof through testing" is one of our group's central mantras. The lessons of Scripture never used to stand out on the page for me as they do now, because the more conscious, intentional practice of my faith has proven those lessons to be relevant, living instruction. I am reminded of Romans 12:18: "Be at peace with your neighbor so far as it is up to you" (as translated by New Testament scholar John Lewis). There will always be incorrigibles in our path—just don't be one of them to someone else. Live the life of Christ with your very best, albeit human effort. And finally, like the parable of the bridesmaids (Matthew 25:1–13), or "The Babes," as I like to call them on Tuesday morning, keep enough of your own powder dry to be ready for the big day coming; the day we call tomorrow.

John McClung, San Antonio, Texas[125]

An Artist Called to Newtown

I am an artist, writer, and Christian educator. I've worked with children, youth, and adults. I've served on staff from very small churches to a very large cathedral. As I began to examine my prayer life more deeply I turned—or shall I say returned—to painting. One night, I put aside my brushes and put my hands directly into the paint. This visceral act enabled me to tap directly into my heart and mind. Painting is the way I talk to God. I find joy when I move my fingers through puddles of color and across blank canvas. I am always surprised and blessed by the conversation that takes place. It is as if a good friend has joined me for a glass of wine and time of catching up.

I now paint at my Grandmother's table, a table I once played under as a child and on which I enjoyed vibrant and delicious meals. The table became a Eucharistic symbol for me. It is the place where I go to paint, pray, and remember. It has become such an important place for me that I knew I had to invite others to the table.

In late March of 2013, I was invited to Trinity Episcopal Church in Newtown, Connecticut, to talk about faith and God with the children and parents of that congregation. Trinity serves many families with children who attended Sandy Hook Elementary School. One of the children of the congregation was one of the children killed on December 14, 2012. The tragedy affected this community in very deep ways.

Once at Trinity, we prepared a large room for offering "The Painting Table."[126] The room was set up with round tables. On each table we had canvas paper, paints, baby wipes, toothpicks, cotton swabs, pencils, writing paper, and scraps of cardboard. Everyone gathered at the tables—mothers with their children, friend with friend, and neighbor with neighbor. We lit a candle, I gave a few instructions, and the painting began. It was an evening of light and love. It was holy ground.

My ministry of painting with others has grown in ways I least expected. I have since shared painting with children whose parents are incarcerated, with mentally challenged individuals, and small groups in a variety of locations. Whether it is through cooking, painting, or Eucharist, we come together to remember. In remembering, we set our eyes to the horizon and go—with verve—out into the world as Christ has called us to do . . . loving and serving the Lord.

Roger Hutchinson, Houston, Texas[127]

A Homemaker Recognizing God's Mission

Over the past several years of reading articles in our parish newsletter about faith connections in the workplace, a common theme I have noticed is that the authors were always surprised to have been contacted and visited by Fletcher Lowe at their workplaces. I was also very surprised when Fletcher called me because at the time I did not have a "workplace." I was a stay-at-home mom. But leave it to Fletcher to think "outside the office"!

My career path up until that point had been winding, with several stops and starts. After college I worked in retail until the birth of my first son, Quint. I then went back to school for my masters in art history (while working part-time). I defended my thesis three weeks after my second son, Peter, was born. I then worked in the museum profession until my daughter Sarah was born. At that point, my husband and I decided that I would stay at home for a while and be "just" a mom. It was during this time that Fletcher contacted me about discussing faith in connection with my workplace.

The life of a stay-at-home mom is filled with activity from morning until night; there is little room for reflection, meditation, or formal prayer. I suppose some nights a few thoughts of faith may have crossed my mind as I fell into bed, exhausted from cooking, cleaning, carpool, grocery shopping, homework help, yard work, errands, volunteer work, and on and on. If I thought then about my faith at all in my "workplace" it was likely in the context of the Martha and Mary story, with myself as a definite Martha!

> But Martha was distracted by her many tasks; so she came to him [Jesus] and asked, "Lord, do you not care that my sister has left me to do all the work by myself? Tell her then to help me." But the Lord answered her, "Martha, Martha, you are worried and distracted by many things; there is need of only one thing. Mary has chosen the better part, which will not be taken away from her." (Luke 10:40–42)

I still feel this way when overwhelmed with tasks. I am no longer a strictly stay-at-home mom (I have been back to work part-time for three years), but as the primary caretaker of my family this happens quite often. However, when looking back on the stay-at-home mom years, it is easier to see from a distance how God's mission was functioning in my daily life and work. I feel that something was allowing me to get through each day relatively unscathed and sane. Perhaps it was the comfort and insight that comes from taking care of others, or the gifts that come with service to others (even one's own family). Even though daily tasks may become routine, there is a beauty in caretaking and trying to do it well. I could see, hear, and touch God in the faces, voices, and hands of my children and husband, and it gave me great peace of mind to know that hopefully by being at home when my children were young, I was giving them the opportunity to grow and learn in an environment I could make for them. Christ was in my workplace and with me in the simple, yet honest, tasks of making a home and rearing my children.

Now back in the workplace as a (paid) museum technician at the Valentine Center, I am working on a project to digitize The Richmond Times-Dispatch *photograph collection held by the Center. My job is solitary, with little interaction with others at the museum—mostly just my computer, scanner, and me. I have plenty of time for reflection— time I did not have when I was at home. It is interesting to think about and experience faith in the context of work now. Each workday I look at many black and white photographs depicting a wide range of subjects relating to the "heart of the city." Many images are routine shots created just for the news story, but others are pieces of art that reflect the beauty and pathos of Christ in everyday life and people. Preserving these images for future generations and doing a job that may make a difference allows me to see my faith connections in the workplace in an expanded light. I am still serving (and caretaking), and still see myself as a Martha, but now my stewardship may potentially influence more people and help other people with their work. Thinking about an often-mundane job in the context of service, preservation, and faith makes it seem almost important.*

My faith manifests itself in the workplace, whether at home or in an office, as service and caretaking. At home, I care for my family by tending to their needs and hopefully allowing them the freedom to grow and become faithful individuals themselves. At work, I am the steward and preserver of one small section of the "heart of the city."

Laura Carr, Richmond, Virginia[128]

A Real Estate Executive Intersecting with Faith

I grew up in a household of faith. Church life was the pivot upon which our weekly schedule turned—and it was the great connector to our closest friends. So conversations about faith were commonplace. During one of these casual conversations, my mother (a saint if ever there was one) offered up this pithy synopsis: "Laura, my faith isn't about fire insurance, it's about what it means to my life here and now." I'm sure my mother has forgotten those words, but I haven't. And as I've grown older, her words have not only echoed in my ears, they have come to represent the fundamentals of my faith. For me, the Christian faith is not about what lies beyond; rather, it is about how we are called to live in the present; and it's about God's abundant grace that invariably, immeasurably enriches our daily lives.

When I consider the question of how we are to live, I return always to the simple, straightforward, yet profoundly challenging command to love one another. For Christians, it is the greatest commandment. But what does that look like? Specifically, a friend asked me recently, how does faith translate into the so-called daily life of the business world?

Always up for some extracurricular theological musings, I was eager to answer that question. Until it dawned on me that an answer would require first a confession: Writing about faith in the business world and living it are two different things. So let me be clear, I am chief among the sinners. In fact, the biblical verse that often resonates most powerfully with me is Paul's acknowledgment in his Letter to the Romans (7:15) that "I do not do what I want, but I do the very thing I hate." So with the proviso that more often than not I fall short, here are some thoughts about the intersection of faith and the daily business grind.

Richmond has been and continues to be blessed with business leaders who are unashamed witnesses to their faith. My first "real" job thirty years ago was as a cashier with Ukrop's supermarket. I still remember my orientation; the touchstone for our corporate culture was the golden rule: Do unto others as you would have them do unto you. More recently, during a meeting of the Richmond Metropolitan Habitat for Humanity Executive Committee, my friend and colleague Imad Damaj arose and quietly asked if there was place in my office he could pray. The time in the day had come to pray and, as a devout Muslim, he heeded the call. No fanfare, no show; just a whisper in my ear. His witness inspires and humbles me—always.

People of faith are not immune from tough, maddening, and saddening business decisions. I've made budget cuts before, I'll make them again. Negotiating fiercely to get the best deal for my members at the lowest cost—that's part of the job description. But I feel compelled to negotiate honestly and transparently; it's the right thing to do, and it turns out to be the best business strategy as well. I have fired employees in the past; I suspect I will do so in the future. But when I do, I am compelled to dismiss people in a way that respects their dignity. I can never forget that these individuals are God's own, created in God's own image.

The world of business is neither isolated nor insulated from the rest of the world. Because of this, business leaders possess ample opportunities to bring about transformative change, especially in the greater community that surrounds their company. In fact, I would suggest that people of faith who are leaders in the business world have a theological imperative to recognize that the world is not as it was created and intended to be, to identify the changes needed to bring about healing and wholeness, and to work without ceasing for change that transforms lives.

I'm not advocating that business leaders use positions of authority to impose their beliefs on others, far from it. But if our faith means anything to us, it must mean something in all aspects of our lives. A worldview informed by faith—in my case the Christian faith, which offers up the most powerful example of agape love and calls us to follow—compels us to understand our corporate responsibilities as part of a larger whole. And with that understanding come consistent civic engagement, tangible acts of service, and generous philanthropy—all of which enhance our common life. The pillar and promise of faith is "give and it will be given to you, good measure, pressed down, running over."

Laura Lafayette, CEO,
Richmond Association of Realtors,
Richmond, Virginia[129]

GOING FORTH

1. *For noticing or sharing with others:* What idea or thought in this chapter caught your imagination, surprised you, challenged your assumptions, inspired you, raised a question, gave you hope, cautioned you, or opened a new perspective? How does that insight relate to your life as a sent Christian?

2. *For analysis:* In addition to those mentioned in this chapter, what essential Christian values would you add to the lists that are important to carry from Sunday into Monday?

3. *For reflection:* What story might you want to tell about living as Christ's ambassador in your own daily life?

4. *For discussion or discernment:* Which of the stories did you find particularly relevant to your own situation? Why? How might that person's experience influence your own faith in daily life?

5. *For action:* Invite two other people to share a bag lunch with you to discuss the connection between faith and daily life.

Roadblocks to Radical Sending

The layperson's ministry is not a matter
of increased busyness in parishes.
Indeed, this proliferation of organizations
and activities may be a roadblock at times
to the realization of lay ministry.
Our ministry is our lives, our total lives.

EDMUND FULLER, NOVELIST AND CRITIC

Richard Halverson, former chaplain to the U.S. Senate 1981–1984, was known for his humorous take on how Christianity has lost focus on "the main thing." Halverson's brief history recounted that Christianity began on Palestinian soil as a relationship with a person. When it moved to Greece, it became a philosophy. When it moved to Rome, it became an institution; when it moved to Britain (or Europe), it became a culture; and when it arrived in America, it became an enterprise.[130] Halverson insisted that the relationship with the person of Jesus was Christianity's essential "main thing." Baptism is our acknowledgement and claiming of that relationship. As the Book of Common Prayer asserts, "You are sealed by the Holy Spirit in Baptism and marked as Christ's own forever" (p. 308).

Fredrica Harris Thompsett offers a more detailed account of the institutional history of the church, relating it to baptism as a mark of belonging:

A Short History of Baptism, or the Tale of the Three Bs—Behaving, Belonging, Believing

Just because you haven't heard of it, doesn't mean it is new!

In the beginning: The baptized are the keepers of the faith, of the gospel, and members of the Pauline body of Christ. "The people of God" is the most used name for the church.

Second to third century: *Behaving* preceded *Belonging* and *Believing*

Fourth century: Era of institutionalization. Christianity under Constantine ordered as religion of the Roman Empire. *Belonging*, but to whom?

Twelfth century: Baptism a necessary sign of *Belonging* with access to salvation.

Sixteenth century: Reformation; baptism is a sign of *Believing* with many different believers.

Seventeenth century: The New World; at first *Belonging* is most important; among the Puritans *Behaving* is the key.

Eighteenth century: The minister was the preacher. Baptisms and funerals in homes.

Nineteenth century: Development of ministry professionals. *Belonging* most important.

1950s and 1960s: Reaction to World War II. Emphasis in the United States on a learned clergy. European emphasis on lay education.

1970s: Liturgical movement places baptism as the beginning of ministry in the context of *Belonging*. Ministers of the church are laity and clergy (bishops, priests, and deacons for Anglican and Catholic traditions).

1980s: A return to baptismal ministry, also known as mutual ministry, shared ministry, local common ministry. Also a return to the Pauline vision of shared ministry. . . . *Believing* in the shared ministry of all shaped the *Belonging*.

NOW: A movement again toward *Behaving* by examining the way we behave in the church and in the world. Observed behavior, rather than knowledge of various beliefs, still attracts converts![131]

Thompsett's analysis parallels the thoughts of Diana Butler Bass, who identifies the shift from the Great Reformation's believing-behaving-belonging paradigm to one of belonging-behaving-believing as a key marker of the postmodern church's return to first-century norms.[132] Bass calls this reordering "The Great Reversal" of the concepts of the past few centuries:

Long ago, before the last half millennium, Christians understood that faith was a matter of community first [belonging], practices second [behaving], and belief as a result of the first two. Our immediate ancestors reversed the order. Now, it is up to us to restore the original order. . . .

Relational community, intentional practice, and experiential belief are forming a new vision for what it means to be Christian in the twenty-first century, a pattern of spiritual awakening that is growing around the world. . . . We are; we act; we know. . . . The Great Reversal is the Great Returning of Christianity back toward what Jesus preached: a beloved and beloving community, a way of life practiced in the world, a profound trust in God that eagerly anticipated God's reign of mercy and justice.[133]

Reclaiming the congregation's identity as a belonging-place, a base camp (a support group, field hospital, campfire, provisioning store for believers) is essential to restoring that order. An identifiable, trustworthy, intentional community of believers provides a base camp where daily-life followers of the way of Jesus can practice recounting stories of their trek as well as (and perhaps as a means of) being renewed and reenergized. As Halverson, Thompsett, and Bass all point out, the last few centuries have fostered a church culture that offers much resistance to a radical shifting in that direction.

Present-Day Church Norms and Expectations

Chief among those cultural norms formed in recent centuries has been the creation of a leadership class of ordained, seminary-trained clergy (*kleros*). Entrance to "the process" that can lead to ordination is typically via a judicatory commission on ministry or other body charged with ensuring that candidates for ordination have been appropriately screened. The source of candidates ultimately recommended for ordination is normally the congregation, which sometimes has a hard time imagining future leaders being any different from present ones. In addition to seminary-trained, ordained priests, larger congregations often have paid professional lay staff as well.

In many church institutions, the voice of professional leadership— particularly clergy—carries far more authority than that of the lay membership, even in nontheological, nonecclesial matters. And in the governing bodies of the church, typically the voting clergy outnumber the laity—despite the ordained comprising 1 percent or less of the typical denomination's membership.[134]

The Struggle for Institutional Survival

In mainline congregations, and increasingly in other denominations, as the average age of the congregation has been rising, the number of funerals is exceeding the number of baptisms and other initiations to membership. In addition to aging, congregations are shrinking (especially the smaller ones), the number of small congregations (membership less than seventy-five people) is growing, and the accepted definition of "faithful Sunday attendance" is moving from four times a month toward two.[135] Dwindling ranks in the pews and dwindling resources—both financial and human—have meant that some congregations have developed a "circle the wagons" mentality, which can contribute to isolation from the community and neighbors that surround them. The Episcopal Church Building Fund,[136] which works with congregations to reframe their understanding and utilization of their assets, often asks participating members to interview homeowners and business people around the church property, asking about their own congregation. A shocking but not unusual response: "Wow, I thought that building was closed."

In the face of such obstacles, church leaders and members are often fearful—of not being able to pay the bills, of having to close the doors, of losing an important element of their faith lives. Often, however, such fears open the doors to the idea of doing something different.

The Sacred and Secular Divide

Many of the norms of church life—norms that were shaped by the "glory days" of twentieth-century culture—have contributed to a growing divide between the sacred and secular. That divide reinforces the view that anything labeled "secular" is of less value than anything understood to be "holy," missing the point entirely that God created the world and judged the whole creation "very good" (Gen. 1:31). Moreover, because God is always present, there is always potential for the holy to show up, especially in unexpected places. That sacred/secular divide allows us to dismiss the daily-life places that people inhabit as essentially unimportant compared to church spaces, the parts of "God's house." As author and pastor Skye Jethani blogs, where the sacred realm is the only one that God cares about, "Accounting . . . is secular work without any eternal value, but doing accounting for a *church*— well, now you're counting beans for the kingdom of God."[137]

Barbara Brown Taylor, an Episcopal priest and theologian, describes the divide this way:

> From the very beginning, being a Christian has meant being a sojourner in a strange land. The reversal in our own day is that for many people it is the church, and not the rest of the world, that is strange. As the moat between the two has widened, the old bridges have become obsolete, leaving commuters to paddle across by themselves the best way they can.[138]

Learning to see God at work in every aspect of our daily lives—in the whole creation—is essential to creating congregations who understand themselves as sent people. Some describe this change as "making the Sunday-to-Monday connection."

Clericalism

Partly because of present-day culture's embrace of specialization and partly because of human sloth, clergy are often regarded as the only "ministers" in a congregation, responsible for all things relating to church. In that role, clergy are seen as "special"; more holy; closer to God; endowed with unparalleled skills, gifts, and insights in all things theological; and, of course, the only person allowed to lead a prayer at any gathering. This super-human image is fostered as much—if not more so—by laity as by clergy. For laity, such an image can absolve them of any agency in church matters, a convenient reason not to take faith and the life of the faith community into their own hands.

The governing institutions of many churches reinforce clericalism when they allow clergy voices and votes to dominate their gatherings. The fact that the body of Christ is overwhelmingly not ordained is often overlooked.

If "God stuff" can only be dealt with by the ordained, then clearly daily life matters are beneath the concern of the church. Such an understanding of the clergy reinforces the sacred-secular divide and damages the faith community.

In December 2013, Pope Francis prayed, "Lord, free your people from a spirit of clericalism and aid them with a spirit of prophecy." He went on to name three themes in the heart of a prophet: "the promise of the past, contemplation of the present and courage to show the way towards the future."[139] Helping clergy and laity to bridge the artificial division of clericalism is critical in empowering people to see themselves as bearers of God's Good News wherever they find themselves.

Homeostasis

My (Demi's) eighth grade biology teacher repeatedly reminded us of the immutable laws of the universe: "God. Motherhood. Apple Pie. And Homeostasis." Mr. Perkins never defined the first three. He described "homeostasis" as the tendency of living things to maintain an internal equilibrium, particularly when faced with external changes. For instance, the human body has developed systems to maintain relatively constant internal temperature, blood volume, and many other factors. Typically, congregations are much the same, preferring consistency over change. In many congregations, much time and energy is expended to ensure that stability is achieved and maintained.

Efforts to change this finely tuned system are uphill battles. In 2004, Loren Mead, once president of the Alban Institute, called lay ministry a lost cause:

> In short we're not dealing with a problem that only resides in our thinking or our programs or processes. We are caught up in a system—an interrelated, interconnected set of relationships that reinforce homeostasis. Anything we do to enhance lay ministry causes a reaction in the system that negates what we do. The system is self-correcting. And it self-corrects back to the same old clergy-centered sense of ministry that we are trying to get away from. . . . We are trying to install an approach that goes against the self-interest of key actors in the system.[140]

Years earlier, in *The Once and Future Church,* Mead warned:

> The rhetoric from the pulpit urges engagement with the world and defines one's "real" ministry as job, community life, family, etc., all of which takes place *outside* the church. Yet the bulletin, the parish organization, the pastor, and staff urge and reward engagement with parish

activities. Ministry outside the church is rarely recognized and never rewarded. Ministry inside is recognized and rewarded.[141]

Now, more than twenty years later, the focus on interior activities has a double edge. For older generations, overcoming homeostasis may mean persuading them to leave the safety of the base camp in order to share God's Good News with those they encounter in their daily lives. Many in younger generations—especially Gen X and younger—may need to see evidence that the congregation has any interest in their daily lives. They may understand themselves as making their trek alone and unsupported, and may need to be persuaded that the congregation is both welcoming and trustworthy. So in both traditional and emerging faith communities the pull of homeostasis may draw the focus inward—whether on the institution or on the individual. The congregation can fail to devote resources to equipping hardy hikers who carry their faith with them into engagement with the wider world.

For both groups, providing "camp fires" where stories can be shared is a powerful tool in overcoming homeostasis, just as Luke 10 says Jesus's disciples experienced when they returned from sharing the Good News.

> When they returned from this first mission, they could not believe what had happened. They discovered that proclaiming the kingdom was not a matter of teaching doctrine; rather, the kingdom was a matter of imitating Jesus's actions. Jesus did not tell them to have faith. He pushed them into the world to practice faith. The disciples did not hope the world would change. They changed it. And in doing so, they themselves changed. . . .
>
> Doing what once seemed difficult or impossible empowers courage to envision a different world and believe we can make a difference.[142]

Even hearing the stories of others doing such difficult or impossible things can ignite the vision of what we—and God—might accomplish together.

God's promise to "do a new thing" is a message of hope when confronting homeostasis in the congregation. The wise leader knows that change always raises anxiety, and that when skillfully managed, anxiety can help create energy for change. Leaders who can develop a toolkit of change management skills can help move a congregation toward becoming a radically sending base camp.

Obstacles to Creating a "Sending" Culture

Given all these challenges, the courage required to do something different—to reframe a congregation's response to its situation, to articulate a new vision—is not easy to come by. And even when leaders are ready to do something different, there are real obstacles to overcome that are embedded in much of church tradition, polity, and history—at least in congregants' memories. Making the daily lives of every member central to the congregation's mission requires a radical reordering of communal life. It is a reordering that grows out of the understanding that belonging to a community of believers is a key support of daily-life behaviors, behaviors that both confirm and proclaim our belief even when our own belief wavers in the storms of our daily lives. As Bob Hibbs, retired bishop suffragan of the Diocese of West Texas, has said, "I need the church. I need the body of Christ to help me recite the Creed and proclaim my belief, especially on those days when I'm not entirely sure I can all by myself."[143]

For many, movement toward becoming a base-camp congregation encounters paralysis and resistance to change—an unwillingness to move out of the "comfort zone"—that grow out of a *lack of vision*. Finding the courage to make the shift toward radical sending is likely to mean:

- Learning and adapting from others' creative solutions—even when they come from outside the usual sources

- Operating without models for this pioneering behavior—and recognizing courage in unlikely people

- Discovering both the power of experimenting—and the bracing experience of learning from our mistakes

- Having to encounter God in the world—and finding the Holy One at work in surprising places

- Surrendering the illusion of control—and broadening the variety of voices we're willing to listen to

- Being criticized or shamed for failing to ask permission, or for "acting on our own"

- Having to encounter "beyond-church" people, "the other," people at the margins—and gaining the wisdom and insight of those who don't share our point of view or privilege or social location

- Sometimes not having "the answer"—or perhaps any answer at all

Those are challenging and yet potentially fruitful possibilities, and our anxieties often arise from our experiences both inside and outside the church. The Good News—that God is right here, right now—is sometimes not enough to overcome the snide criticism and the fear of failure that can accompany doing "a new thing." Jesus did say, "I have said this to you, so that in me you may have peace. In the world you face persecution. But take courage; I have conquered the world!" (John 16:33).

On another front, for those who are "church insiders" (both laity and clergy), becoming a base-camp congregation seems to violate *tradition* and *polity* as we know it, raising reactive defenses. The radically sending base camp model seems to fly in the face of the creature comforts of:

- The tendency to identify those who work in the church or who hold advanced theological degrees as somehow "closer to God"

- Our reliance on ordained leadership, whether we do so out of convenience, lack of engagement, or deference to their status

- Our habit of training ordained leadership to manage and control, rather than to facilitate ministry, without acknowledging the wealth of training, gifts, and education among the congregation

- Our inclination to think of ministry as being church (building) based, which fails to recognize God's presence and action in all the world

- For liturgical churches, a reliance on customs of rite and ceremony that keep our corporate worship inwardly focused, often decreasing opportunities for imaginative engagement and broader participation

- Our overemphasis on human unworthiness, without a complementary emphasis on being cocreators with God, a key tenet of baptismal theology that has not been widely incorporated into Christian formation

Finally, the *inadequacy of spiritual formation* provided in the context of many congregations is a source of paralysis among the rank and file. With the dissolution of Christendom and the shift to a post-Christendom culture, those who have already been shaped by a healthy Christian community are increasingly unable to appreciate how spotty Christian acculturation has become, both for children and adults. And for those lacking such formation, it is difficult to know what might be missing.

Followers of the Way of Jesus are particularly susceptible to feeling inadequate to be bearers of God's Good News whenever they lack a solid foundation in:

- Understanding and incarnating the priesthood of all believers—the source of liberation to act as Christ's ambassadors in our daily lives

- Recognizing that baptism joins us with Christ in God's mission—the commissioning to be bearers of God's Good News

- Knowing with conviction what is God's Good News—the assurance that our loving God is here with us

- Accepting that the most important tools of evangelism are attraction and imitation, not authoritative theology

- Reclaiming the first-century process of belonging-behaving-believing

- Adopting the essentials of faithful practice—those time-tested, faith-building habits that harness the formational power of behaving

- Being open to living in the paradox of God as both immanent and transcendent—nearer than breathing and at the same time beyond the limits of knowledge and experience

- Being willing to be blessed by Christ's compassion, especially manifest in his tenderness, his fierceness, and his playfulness[144]

All of these obstacles to creating a sending culture—fed at least in part by resistance, reactivity, and lack of both vision and formation—work against imaginative thinking, which in times past was often seen as an undesirable trait. As the church, along with the rest of civilization, negotiates what Phyllis Tickle has called "The Great Emergence,"[145] congregations and church institutions will need to intentionally engage the corporate imagination. That imagination can inspire congregations to join the great adventure, to live prophetically in a way that testifies to a new creation, and to "put on Christ," leading to transformation of ourselves and the world.

GOING FORTH

1. *For noticing or sharing with others:* What idea or thought in this chapter caught your imagination, surprised you, challenged your assumptions, inspired you, raised a question, gave you hope, cautioned you, or opened a new perspective? How does that insight relate to your life as a sent Christian?

2. *For analysis:* What among the roadblocks named in the chapter are obstacles in your own congregation? Are there others not named that you see?

3. *For reflection:* What "new thing" discussed in this chapter do you find most frightening or disturbing? How might God be lovingly calling you to examine that obstacle in your own life?

4. *For discussion or discernment:* How might your congregation increase a sense of "belonging" among all the people who come into contact with you? How might your congregation encourage people to move from "belonging" to "behaving"?

5. *For action:* Write a prayer that asks God's deliverance from at least one roadblock hindering your congregation. Pray the prayer each day for a week, and reflect on what you're noticing.

✝

PART III

The Practice of
Radical
Sending

Shifts in Perspective

Why did we ever leave Egypt?

(Numbers 11:20c)

Anybody can observe the Sabbath, but
making it holy surely takes the rest of the week.

Alice Walker, *In Search of Our Mothers' Gardens*

Your congregation may discern that the next best step is developing a radically sending "base camp" culture. If so, then prepare to enter a transition zone. In many cases, the transition is less one of substance than perception. The bottom line for all participants may be to stop trying harder and doing more. We might all be better served by doing a bit less and reflecting a bit more on the meaning and impact of what we are doing.

Our culture is shifting around us. (Some would say, at least of the Church, that the culture is shifting not just "around us," but "way ahead of us.") The Age of Enlightenment, with its emphasis on rational process, and the Industrial Age, with its emphasis on institutions and machines to solve problems, have given way to the Information Age, where data—not all of it accurate—floods our lives and our homes via platforms undreamt of twenty years ago. This cultural shift has transformed many of our workplaces, in particular, from top-down bureaucracies to less-structured, team-driven, interactive, and interdependent enterprises. Most of the people who come in contact with our faith communities spend much of their lives in this transformed world. For them, in their working lives, "The World Is Flat,"[146] as Thomas L. Friedman's popular 2005 book detailed. They tend to

109

have open workspaces, not private offices. Their workday interactions are driven by connectional networking rather than hierarchical or committee-dominated structures. They value team-driven response and innovation over command-and-control.

Their daily lives are mostly spent in environments that are at best neutral and at worst actively hostile to religions, including Christianity, if not to God's Good News. Unlike church officials and employees—whose day-to-day interactions are largely with church members, clergy, and spiritual seekers—most church members deal daily with "all sorts and conditions" of human beings, who hail from all over the landscape and whose code of behavior may or may not be grounded in the gospel or any other religious guidelines for living.

The people who understand themselves as church "insiders" operate in a culture that is quite different from the one that church-going "outsiders" encounter, and the gap is rarely discussed. However, it undoubtedly shapes differing understandings of what God's Good News has to do with everyday life and how everyday people participate in what God is up to in the world.

A New Vision: Church as Radically Sending Base Camp

Reframing, reimagining our understanding of how "church" functions in the lives of members and the community can lead to bridging that cultural gap. The "base camp" congregation that we're envisioning—and beginning to see realized in congregations—understands itself as the place where:

- All hikers—especially "the other"—are welcome (the "radical welcome" element);

- All are expected to go out—sent by the Lord Jesus—to embody God's Good News, to live their faith in the world beyond the congregation's doors (the "radical sending" element);

- Those who go out as bearers of Good News are celebrated on their return, and encouraged to share the story of their journey, including the bumps along the way and where they saw God at work (the "transformational storytelling" element);

- Leaders understand themselves as servants (the "servant leadership" element).

Please note that we are purposefully not focusing on congregational outreach as a "base camp" practice because it is still church centered and organized. We are focused on the radical sending of the baptized into their own worlds of daily life beyond the church grounds.

The mission of the radically sending congregation therefore is not centered on serving the members and attracting more to join. Instead, it is aimed toward equipping, supporting, and inspiring all who are touched by the congregation's focus to go forth bearing God's Good News. Just like those sent out by Jesus in Luke 10, present-day bearers of Good News embody in their daily lives the truth that God is already present wherever we are and that God loves us (including all creation). While the congregation does seek to nourish, heal, shelter, and strengthen, it understands the special role of stories in its congregate life, especially the stories from members' daily lives. The hikers experience hills and valleys and straight places on their daily journeys. Their shared stories connect their faith with their daily lives—transforming for both hearers and bearers of the Good News and generating inspiration, encouragement, forgiveness, determination, and energy to go forth yet again. The congregation may pay some individuals, but not to "do ministry," because the members understand that a calling to ministry is not a task but our baptismal identity in Christ. Instead, those who are paid understand that they are to facilitate the ministries of others.

These guideposts—radical welcome, radical sending, transformational storytelling, and servant leadership—are all hallmarks of Jesus's ministry. For that reason, they are truly radical—at the very root of our tradition and our faith. In radically sending congregations, all of them are embodied in the essential functions of the gathered congregation: formation, liturgy, pastoral care, and communication. Succeeding chapters will detail some of the strategies for using those functions to reinforce "base camp" thinking. Those strategies can help reshape the congregation's understanding of itself and its mission. Before those strategies can be put to work, there are some key shifts that are foundational.

Practicing Radical Welcome

Unfortunately, in the minds of much of the world, the church has all too often defined itself by those it excluded, considering them unworthy to take part in its communal life. Nearly a decade ago, Stephanie

Spellers, in her book *Radical Welcome*,[147] called on churches to practice instead a radical hospitality in response to the work of God—the God of relationship, of transformation, and of welcome. She challenged churches to be converted, to enter into a spiritual practice of radical welcome. She painted a picture of congregations—those brave enough to move beyond being merely inviting and inclusive—that were transformed by joyfully accepting the gift of "the other" in their midst. Her book charts a course for a congregation to examine its mission and vision, its identity, its ministries and relationships, its leadership and feedback systems, and its worship, all in light of the question: "Where is God calling us?" While recognizing the power of fear to thwart change in the congregation, she counsels intentionality, purposeful discernment, openness, and incrementalism.

In concluding her persuasive case for congregations learning to be genuinely open-hearted, Spellers writes:

> Can we faithfully make room for each other's gifts, voices and images to shape worship? Can we grow to trust each other's skills for leadership? Can we allow our identities to be converted by the encounter with The Other? Can we partner for ministry as equally beloved but differently gifted children of God? Can we make intentional, systemic efforts to open our communities in these ways, knowing that transformation rarely emerges as a byproduct of comfortable, one-shot programs? And can we do all these things trusting that Christ will show up more powerfully, smiling and beckoning us deeper into this radical call?[148]

She ends with a bold mandate for authentic change:

> Are we the gathering of God's radically open, radically loving, radically welcoming people? Then we should make it abundantly clear that we are the least stiff, least unforgiving, least crusty, least homogenous, least fearful, least judgmental people in the world. If our public personae say otherwise, then we must take seriously the call to become an indisputably, radically welcoming presence in our communities.[149]

Authentic welcome cannot be faked, and it cannot be limited to a recognized, "members only" group. A shift toward the practice of radical welcome paves the way for the congregation to claim its radical sending identity. Its ability to function as a base camp depends on its being truly open to serve the needs of the "hikers," who are bearers of God's Good News in their daily lives. Spellers's powerful case for radical welcome leads directly into radical sending. It is the welcoming congregation that equips and prepares and nurtures and affirms its members as they "go forth to love and serve the Lord" in their everyday worlds.

Promoting Partnership among All the Baptized

Opening the doors of the church to radical sending entails opening the community's understanding of who might be welcome to act as a bearer of God's Good News and how baptism equips all to claim the ministry of the baptized in their daily lives.

Fletcher asked this question in *Baptism: The Event and the Adventure*, as well as offering a response:

> How do we enhance the calling of the baptized so they don't have to become clergy to be authentically Christian, as if joining the ranks of the ordained is the only true way to be fully a follower?
>
> The vision would cause a total refocusing of the church's life away from the church as institution to the church as equipper of the baptized for their ministry in the world of work and family and community and leisure; where what the baptized do Monday-to-Saturday is seen as having as much to do about faith as what is done on Sunday; where the plumber's call is seen as just as significant as that of the ordained; where the real locus of faith is exercised at the desk and the bench and the sink and the tractor as well as the altar. That we continue to expend as much precious institutional energy over the ordination of women and gays is illustrative of the systemic problem. In so doing we further downgrade the ministry of all the baptized by raising the bar of ordination, reinforcing the clericalism that distorts the true mission of the Church.
>
> In our clericalism, our focus on ordination, we lose sight of the preposterous calling of our baptism and its outrageous claims upon us including doing God's work in the market place. As expressed by the ELCA, "Take a baptized Christian, empowered by the Gospel, thrown into the world and watch what happens." Something Theodore Eastman, retired bishop of the Diocese of Maryland, calls "walking wet!"
>
> A systemic change needs to be implemented at the top. That includes some reprogramming of bishops and clergy, diocesan structures, especially commissions on ministry, national church bodies,

seminaries, etc.—in short a call to revolution, just as significant as the Constantinian revolution centuries ago that began the clericalism march. In many situations this would call for a radical reorientation of the congregation's life and focus. In short a congregation would supply the hiker with whatever he/she needs of nourishment, reflection, encouragement, equipment for the weekly journey out from the camp onto the mountain. The ordained become, as one among the baptized, one of the many persons called to provide, supply, equip, encourage, affirm, and support the hikers in their journey.[150]

Sue Mallory, a lay Presbyterian and founding executive director of Leadership Training Network, worked tirelessly to empower her congregation's lay members in their callings. Describing her congregation, she wrote:

We really struggled to put into action the discovery that our pastor wasn't supposed to know and do everything. As long as our [congregation's] culture operated under the assumption that the pastor *could* do everything, the corollary was that we could do nothing. If, however, the Bible passages that describe the church as an organism speak the truth, then the idea of the all-purpose, all-sufficient, all-knowing, all-doing pastor must be wrong. We knew there had to be a healthier, more biblical way to do ministry than the way our culture was dictating.[151]

In the same vein, Lutheran pastor Judith McWilliams Dickhart's chart "The Roles of Clergy and Laity Inside and Out"[152] (referenced in the previous chapter "In Their Own Words") presents a clear picture of well-worn assumptions contrasted with a more life-giving "new angle." She calls on all Christians—laity and clergy—to function as ministers full-time, both inside and outside the church.

For this shift to succeed, laity and clergy alike will need to let go of some of the long-held ideas about what the church needs to deliver. The congregation will need to learn to value imagination as well as predictability; experimentation as well as good order; and failure—when learnings are put to work—as well as success. Messiness is often a necessary component of life-giving communal work. As Genesis reminds us, God *did* use chaos as the raw material for the whole created world.

Facilitating Systemic Change

Back in 1993, authors R. Paul Stevens and Phil Collins wrote:

> For more than thirty years the Western church has been exposed
> to a growing number of books and resources focused on the release
> of every member of the church for ministry and mission . . . [but]
> this proliferation of information has produced very little change in
> church life.[153]

Even after the passage of an additional twenty years, the situation
appears to be substantially unchanged, as congregations continue to
focus on their internal lives and services to those understood to be
"members." As Stevens and Collins prescribed, "The most direct way
to equip the saints for the work of ministry is not to devise strategies
for equipping individuals but to equip the church (as a system). Then
the church will equip the saints."[154]

Their excellent, undercelebrated book offers a short-course on systems thinking, as well as ten tactics for shifting systemic norms. They
describe the essential elements of the process as "envisioning, cultivating the environment, and making changes systemically. . . . Process
leadership asks questions, clarifies goals, orients people to their mission, maintains and explains the culture, and helps families and other
sub-congregations take responsibility for their own systemic life."[155]

Before putting forward specifics, the authors offer this caution:

> To blame the frozen state of the layperson on the clergy is far too
> simple and unkind. The nonclergy portion of the laity cannot be lib-
> erated or empowered simply by telling the clergy to move over and
> make room for the layperson. Nor will it happen simply by telling
> laypeople to move up and become one of the ministers of the church.
> We are dealing with complex historical forces that have impinged on
> the church's life over several centuries, forces that were only partially
> resisted by the Protestant Reformation. It is a systemic problem and it
> requires a systemic solution.[156]

They go on to present "ten principles for systems equippers":

1. Work with the Whole
2. Cultivate Healthy Interdependence among Members
3. Lead the Process Not the People
4. Cultivate the Culture

5. Make Changes Slowly and Indirectly

6. Sound Your Own Vision and Define Yourself

7. Shepherd the System and the Subsystems

8. Avoid Becoming Triangled

9. Maintain Open Boundaries with the World

10. Relax: The Church Is in Good Hands[157]

Applying those principles to the congregational system can lead to liberating the laity to be Christ's ambassadors in the world—all of it, both outside and inside the congregation. Leaders within the congregation can work to create a radically sending culture, but without a shift in the system their efforts are unlikely to produce significant, lasting change.

Examining the Unspoken Curriculum

John Westerhoff, Episcopal priest and prolific author, persistently warns about the power of "the unspoken curriculum," the often-unarticulated lessons taught by our customs, our behaviors, and our assumptions. The proportion of any congregation that attends Christian formation—Sunday school classes, seminars, discussion groups, and trainings—is only a small percentage of those who attend worship, especially among the adults. By far, the formation received by adults in any congregation is imparted during worship.

Certainly the sermon is considered an essential component of that teaching. But what is taught in the worship itself, outside of the time spent listening to the preacher? And what lessons are learned implicitly from:

- Who speaks during worship?
- What uniform is worn by which worshippers, and what does each uniform "teach"?
- Who exercises power or control during the time of worship, and in what forms?
- What is the role of clergy before and after the worship?
- What does our worship space and our worship furniture say about our image of God?

- Who stands and sits where, and why?

- What vocations receive attention—or even mention—during worship?

- What activities are commended during worship?

- Who do we pray for?

It's daunting to recognize that each action, practically each word, in worship carries a message not only about God but also about our relationships and our roles both within and outside our faith community. Posing such questions doesn't indicate that the customs and traditions of a congregation need wholesale change. Encouraging mindfulness about what we say even when we're not speaking is essential. Articulating the meanings of our traditions and customs can be transformational.

Creating a radically sending "base camp" culture, where all God's people understand themselves as agents of God's mission, may be enhanced by shifts in the lessons we unconsciously teach when the community gathers.

Reclaiming the Theology of Vocation

"We are a sent people. We don't wait for someone to send us out and then we go; we're already there."[158] This remark (from a church leader) applies equally to all the baptized. Centuries of institutional church practice have eroded the understanding of "call," so that in ordinary conversation the statement "I think I have a vocation" is understood to mean "I believe I am called to be ordained."

Barbara Brown Taylor urges that we reframe the word "vocation":

What many Christians are missing in their lives is a sense of vocation. The word itself means a call or summons, so that having a vocation means more than having a job. It means answering a specific call. . . . it means participating in the work of God, something that few lay people believe they do. . . .

[Luther] made careful distinction between a Christian's vocation and a Christian's office, suggesting that our offices are what we do for a living—teacher, shopkeeper, homemaker, priest—and that none of them is any dearer to the heart of God than another. In our offices we exercise the diversity of our gifts, playing our parts in the ongoing life of the world. Our offices are the "texts" of our lives, to use a dramatic term, but the "subtext" is the common vocation to which we are all called at baptism. Whatever our individual offices in the world, our mutual vocation is to serve God through them. . . .

Perhaps we should revive Luther's vision of the priesthood of all believers, who are ordained by God at baptism to share Christ's ministry in the world—a body of people united by that one common vocation, which they pursue across the gamut of their offices in the world. It is a vision that requires a rich and disciplined imagination, because it is largely a matter of learning to see in a different way. To believe in one's own priesthood is to see the extraordinary dimensions of an ordinary life, to see the hand of God at work in the world and to see one's own hands as necessary to that work. Whether those hands are diapering an infant, assembling an automobile or balancing a corporate account, they are God's hands, claimed by God at baptism for the accomplishment of God's will on earth.[159]

Often, embroiled in the details of daily living, laypeople have difficulty connecting the values they hear proclaimed in church with the values of their daily lives, where they, in Luther's terms, exercise their "office." In his book *The Monday Connection*, Bill Diehl, a Bethlehem Steel sales manager for thirty-two years, named five ways that laypeople incarnate God's work in the world (what Diehl termed "ministry") in their daily lives: competency, presence, ethics, change, and lived values.[160] Diehl worked to raise awareness among those who were not ordained that they were partnering with God "for the accomplishment of God's will on earth," as Taylor described it. Working a similar pattern as the one described in the earlier chapter on "Servants in Daily Life," Diehl shaped his conversations with laypeople around three questions:

1. What do you do?

2. What are the decisions and the problems you have to face in what you do?

3. How do you see your faith relating to these problems and decisions?[161]

These are key questions in perceiving vocation. And all too often, the church has not asked its people to consider them, at least in terms of their daily lives. No wonder it's challenging to imagine having "a vocation" outside the church walls.

Episcopal priest Dwight Zscheile affirms, "Today's new apostolic era calls us back to a much more expansive view, where every member is a missionary in daily life,"[162] citing the work of Wayne Schwab and Member Mission Network and their tools for helping laity claim their mission fields. Zscheile goes on to frame vocation, or calling, as a concern not only for individuals but for the faith community as a body—the body of Christ:

> The shape of God's communal life with and for the world must define the shape of the church's life with and for the world in God's image. . . . Our calling is to discern how we might faithfully share in God's renewing movement in our neighborhoods and world according to the gifts God has given us, in the power of the Spirit, *with* our very humanity. Reconciliation and salvation are God's work in, through, and beyond us—not our task to accomplish on God's behalf.[163]

Reclaiming this expansive, individual, and communal understanding of vocation is an important shift that increases each Christian's identity and agency as a bearer of Good News. Stevens and Collins quote Elton Trueblood proclaiming, "You cannot go to church; you are the church wherever you go." And they offer a hopeful vision: "Constitutionally, the church is an outcropping of the kingdom of God that penetrates this present age like salt, light, fire, keys, and yeast. The church *is* mission. It does not 'have' missions as one of its many optional activities."[164] The good news is that we don't have to take God anywhere. God is already there, present and acting, wherever we "live and move and have our being." Radical sending—our call, our vocation, our mission, and our ministry—is to be "the Christ" in our daily lives where God already is. Modeling its vocation as a called community, and forming individuals to understand themselves as called and sent, the "radically sending" congregation shifts its identity away from "church as destination" (the church gathered) and toward "church engaged in the world" (the church scattered).

GOING FORTH

1. *For noticing or sharing with others:* What idea or thought in this chapter caught your imagination, surprised you, challenged your assumptions, inspired you, raised a question, gave you

hope, cautioned you, or opened a new perspective? How does that insight relate to your life as a sent Christian?

2. *For analysis:* What do you see as the most important shift your congregation might need to make in order to move toward becoming a "sending congregation"?

3. *For reflection:* What do you find most energizing or exciting about the vision of your own congregation as a base camp? Why?

4. *For discussion or discernment:* Where in your faith community's life together can the members share stories of God at work around and through them beyond the church walls? How might God be moving in your congregation and/or the larger church to increase God's people's understanding of call and vocation?

5. *For action:* Write a "mission statement" for your own life that takes into account what you believe God wants for your life.

Making the Transitions

The life-and-death question for each of our
churches and denominations may boil down to this:
are we a club for the elite who pretend to have arrived
or a school for disciples who are still on the way?

BRIAN MCLAREN, *FINDING OUR WAY AGAIN*

We can't say this often enough: The local congregation is the key to enhancing the ministry and mission of the baptized in their daily lives. The congregation is the base camp upon which the hikers depend for their encouragement, nurture, equipping, and affirmation as they move out onto their treks in their worlds of home and community and job and leisure. In short, how could a congregation's life be a radically sending base camp for its members; not the destination but the launching pad, the way station, the place of replenishment providing spiritual nurture for each member's daily hikes? When the congregation serves as base camp, every Sunday each of us is nourished and fed for our Monday-Saturday journey, with the Dismissal as our marching orders—our radical sending into the world.

Getting Started

The key question for getting started is: Who are *you* in your congregation? The ordained leadership? A lay leader? A member of the congregation feeling a need for support for your own daily life ministry? The answer to that will determine what comes next.

121

Situation 1:

You are the ordained leadership. You initiate the idea. It is essential for the lay leadership to share your vision. Once some of the lay leadership buy into becoming a radical sending congregation, you will need to gather a small group to explore possibilities for the congregation. For Episcopalians, this is the most straightforward scenario because in our structure, the ordained command such authority and influence. However, for such a shift to become an enduring part of the congregation's life together, a significant portion of the lay leadership must have ownership.

Situation 2:

You are one of the lay leaders in your congregation and you want to initiate a shift toward "radical sending." This is where purposeful and frequent conversations with the ordained leadership are necessary to share the vision and win clergy support. Gathering a small group of laity and clergy to explore possibilities for the congregation can help your vision gain traction.

Situation 3:

You are a member of the congregation who has the vision of a "radical sending" congregation, and you want to share it with the rest of your faith community. (This is both the most common and the most challenging scenario.) Gather a small group to begin developing allies. As you explore possibilities for the congregation, be sure to share your ideas with lay and clergy leadership. Of course a group of laity can choose to pursue this vision outside of their congregation. Gaining support from the congregation's leaders will increase your effectiveness.

Regardless of your situation as noted above, forming a small group is key to making the needed transitions and then going deeper and climbing higher. And, note well, resistance often comes from this vision being seen as another "program" to be added to an already full agenda and/or as undermining the institutional-church view that lay ministry is what laypeople do to help the congregation/base camp run, for example, the altar guild, vestry, or church school.

Assessing Where You Are: "Mind the Gap"

A number of railway transit systems offer warnings reminding passengers to "mind the gap"—meaning, be careful that you don't trip as you enter and exit, navigating the gap between the platform and the cars. As you work to share a base camp vision with your congregation and your friends, be sure to "mind the gap" between current culture and a base camp mindset; between accustomed roles and new, reframed ones; between inward-focused values and those of radical sending.

The previous chapter listed five major shifts that are important for each congregation to navigate in order to become a healthy, well-functioning base camp:

- Practicing radical welcome
- Promoting partnership among all the baptized
- Facilitating systemic change
- Examining the unspoken curriculum
- Reclaiming the theology of vocation

As your group gathers, you will find it helpful to take stock of your congregation's strengths and challenges in those five areas. Successfully engaging the strategies suggested in the remainder of this chapter will depend on building up your strengths and fostering growth in the areas that need development.

Growing the Radical Sending Vision: The Core Group

Essential to growing the vision of your congregation as a base camp will be gathering a group of people to share thoughts, prayers, and experiences, as well as to learn about the theological grounding and developmental possibilities for radical sending. Regardless of your position in the congregation, the systemic and cultural changes in becoming a base camp are "village work." The congregation itself will need to participate in its own transformation, both in planning and in execution. These changes simply cannot be accomplished by one person's effort.

Building a small group to lay the foundations for this work is very similar to starting any ministry. The group itself will need to develop norms for discerning how its life will be directed. As the group lives and learns and grows together, draw on the following recommendations to shape the formation of a capable core group that can guide the congregation:

Gather the Group

You may want to begin small, "by invitation only." But it's important to create a group that is open to welcoming those who share your passion for becoming a radically sending congregation. Probably six to twelve in the core group is a good number.

Given your particular situation, try to build diversity into your group by including a spectrum of voices in your conversations. Invite people to come to explore with you how the congregation might begin to focus on its call to "equip the saints for the work of ministry" in their daily lives (Eph. 4:12).

When you first meet, be sure to spend time allowing people to tell what they do and how they sense their work to be a calling. Remember that full-time paid work in an office is only one setting for people's daily lives.

Study Key Texts Together

We hope you'll want to use this book (especially "The Base Camp," beginning on page 19) as a focus for your study. In addition, be sure to spend time with Luke 10:1–12 and Ephesians 4:1–7, 11–16. The "Dwelling in the Word"[165] process utilized by Church Innovations can be particularly helpful.

Open Paths for Personal Discovery

Growing in understanding about gifts, your own and the gifts of others, builds confidence in the wealth of capabilities in the congregation. Some congregations utilize spiritual gifts assessments; other find that more "secular" instruments (StrengthsFinders, Myers-Briggs Type Indicator, DiSC® Personality Profile, and many others) lead to more "daily life friendly" applications. Such tests are often used in the context of the workplace to encourage team formation and functioning.

Develop Leaders' Skills in Managing Change

Becoming more skillful in self-differentiation and cultivating a "less anxious presence" are leadership skills that allow change agents to remain focused. The work of authors like Peter Steinke[166] and Gil Rendle[167] can offer helpful guidance. Your small group can be catalytic in helping the leaders in your congregation become more skillful, especially by opening the doors to leadership wisdom from secular-world experts like Jim Collins[168] and Ron Heifetz.[169]

Use Your Radical Welcome Skills to Broaden Your Congregation's Diversity and Reach

Take advantage of your congregation's developing culture of radical welcome to tap the experiences of diverse social, economic, ethnic, language, and age groups. Remember that a base camp culture may well open the doors to people who otherwise might not feel welcome, especially younger generations who may be skeptical of the church's interest in their daily lives.

Commit Yourself in Your Own Daily Life to Be Christ's Presence in Your Workplace

We can't give away what we don't already have. So commit yourselves as a group to exploring your own ministries in all areas of your life—home, workplace, community, wider world, leisure, spiritual development, and church community. Member Mission Network's work is especially helpful.[170] And remember Bill Diehl's five examples of ways that the baptized incarnate ministry in daily life: competency, presence, ethics, change, and lived values.[171]

Form Listening Teams to Work with Occupational Groups

In order to broaden their understanding of different workplace cultures, the members of Colchester Federated Church formed a three-person "listening team." That group invited occupational groups—people in health care, or municipal government, or education, for instance—to gather for an evening of conversation about their work and the issues they faced. In her book *The Empowering Church*, Pastor Davida Foy Crabtree describes those conversations and the impact on her congregation's commitment to support laypeople's ministries in the world.[172] The process allowed increased input from working class and less verbally skilled people, and expanded the thinking not only of the listening team but also of the group implementing the shift to functioning as a more empowering church.

Remember the Shifts in Community Life That You're Seeking to Cultivate

The group will shape its plan of work by assessing how the congregation needs to promote those shifts in thinking listed in the previous chapter.

Pray for One Another, for Your Congregation, and for Individuals in Their Workplaces

We believe that prayer changes us as well as the circumstances we face, and draws us closer to the heart of God. Remember the power of individual and corporate prayer, and encourage one another to develop an intentional discipline of deepening your spiritual lives. Corinne Ware's *St. Benedict on the Freeway* can offer ways to use Benedict's hours of prayer to bridge gaps between our secular lives and the sacred.[173]

Transition into new ways of thinking will take time. Just remember to make use of the group process tools listed above. Keep aiming toward these shifts in thinking as the focus of your core group's long-term strategy and a consistent part of your congregation's life together:

- Practicing radical welcome
- Promoting partnership among all the baptized
- Facilitating systemic change
- Examining the unspoken curriculum
- Reclaiming the theology of vocation

The base camp that your congregation creates will be distinctive to your time and place. The small core group you build will be the starting ground from which base camp culture can infect every aspect of the congregation's life. In the next chapter, we'll offer "seed ideas" for ways that you can make radical sending a part of your congregation's life when you gather to worship, as you form one another in the faith, when you care for one another, and as you communicate about your congregation's life and work.

GOING FORTH

1. *For noticing or sharing with others:* What idea or thought in this chapter caught your imagination, surprised you, challenged your assumptions, inspired you, raised a question, gave you hope, cautioned you, or opened a new perspective? How does that insight relate to your life as a sent Christian?

2. *For analysis:* Whom in your congregation do you need as allies in discerning how your congregation might be called to be a "sending congregation"? How will you invite them into the process?

3. *For reflection:* In building your small group, what or who is God calling you to focus on?

4. *For discussion or discernment:* How will you know you're ready to "go public" with your vision of a base camp congregation? How will you celebrate the "launch"?

5. *For action:* Target a specific "small-step" milestone that your group wants to achieve and plan your team's celebration when you've reached it.

Climbing Higher

Let nothing disturb you.

Let nothing frighten you.

All things pass. God does not change.

Patience achieves everything.

Whoever has God lacks nothing.

God alone suffices.

TERESA OF ÁVILA

As you have moved through this book, you may have wondered, where do I go from here? If your congregation is moving along on the ministry in daily life road, what other resources are there to continue to support and stretch your congregation? If your congregation is not that far, but you feel a calling to move it along, you may be wondering, how do I get this ship underway? What follows is our attempt to provide some of that guidance. In doing so we are drawing on pioneering work by several of our colleagues whose experience can benefit us all on this journey. As Jack Fortin, a Lutheran friend, recently commented:

> I do see signs of hope. It's not a question of those who "get it." It's a much more humble approach. . . .We need models of hope, what I call "friendly experiments." . . . The key is to engage in friendly experiments, and recognize that we're all trying to figure it out. There is no one formula. . . . It's walking, and then talking about it.[174]

You are that sign of hope. With your small core group, explore possibilities for your congregation to develop a radical sending culture. Remember, though, that it is *your* congregation, and you need to tailor

the process in light of *your* congregation, *your* "friendly experiments."
Below is a cafeteria of tested "seed" ideas for your congregation to try
out as possibilities or as springboards for your own imagination. The
suggestions focus on four major areas that require the energy of the
gathered community: Christian formation, liturgy, pastoral care, and
communication. The goal is to offer nourishment that can be carried
into the many daily-life venues where members of your congregation
spend their time, and have the opportunity to be bearers of Good
News, just like those early disciples that Jesus sent out to proclaim,
"The kingdom of God has come near to you" (Luke 10:9).

Engaging Christian Formation

Ideally, in order to move the congregation toward more effectively
functioning as a base camp, the main emphasis in all Christian formation programming and scheduling—for children, youth, and adults—
focuses on nurturing, equipping, supporting, and strengthening all
members in their daily journeys at work, family, school, and community. Some of the possibilities for programs and events that you can
use to move toward a radical sending culture include:

- A short adult study series, focusing on a particular book or Scripture, or on one of the developmental issues your core small
  group has targeted as needing work. (See chapter "Making the
  Transitions" and appendix A: Practicing for the Climb)

- A critical incident weekday lunch group, determined either by
  profession or by geography. Such groups typically discuss workplace issues brought by participants, and seek not to solve the
  issue but to broaden awareness of appropriate, Gospel-based responses. See appendix A for possibilities.

- Case studies on situations in daily life for discussion on Sunday
  mornings or in other faith-formation settings. Certainly these
  can be incidents drawn from real life. One congregation, Colchester Federated Church in Colchester, Connecticut, crafted
  "updated" scenarios drawn from Scripture to engage timeless
  issues in contemporary settings.[175]

- A retreat or intensive study. Having laity—particularly those who
  are not on the church payroll—as presenters offers an opportunity to work against the forces of homeostasis and clericalism.

This can provide an important opportunity for expanding the influence of your core small group in sharing the "base camp" message. See appendix A for an outline and www.RadicalSending.com for a full process.

- A series on the biblical meaning of ministry in the Old and New Testaments. Passages like Luke 10:1–2 and Ephesians 4:1–7, 11–16 can be particularly fruitful, along with Philippians 2:1–11 and Exodus 18:13–24.

- Group studies that move from life to Scripture. At least initially, taking a news item or life situation as the starting point requires a resource person who is conversant with Scripture, in order to direct participants to stories that apply. Using this process, participants at The Work+Shop[176] in San Antonio, Texas, rapidly increased their biblical literacy as well as their ability to see their workplace through a gospel lens.

- A series on ways in which Christians throughout the centuries and in our own day have lived out their ministry in the world.

- Opportunities to explore the meaning of baptism, the Baptismal Covenant, and living into one's call as the baptized in the world. See chapters "The Base Camp" and "So I Send You" for possibilities.

- Gifts identification is a means to help members of the congregation identify and claim their gifts. It is important for the study to inspire participants to continue to develop and use their gifts in their daily lives, and to provide ways to have them affirmed by the congregation. Utilizing more "secular" instruments that are commonly used in the workplace such as StrengthsFinders, DiSC® Personality Profile, and Myers-Briggs Type Indicator, rather than more faith-based tests can be a powerful way to link Monday-Saturday life to Sunday.

Transformational Liturgy

Especially for those of us who worship with some regularity, it's easy to forget the power of liturgy to teach and to form our ideas in nonverbal ways. As mentioned in the chapter on "Shifts in Perspective," the unspoken curriculum taught when the community gathers for worship carries often-unrecognized authority in shaping our ideas about God, ministry, and how we are to live our lives on a day-to-day basis. The up side is that even subtle shifts in liturgy can be especially effective in forming a radical sending congregation.

- Examine how the readings, the music, the sermons, and the prayers Sunday-after-Sunday point to the doors—that is, to the "dismissal" moment when the congregation is sent out into the world to be bearers of God's Good News. This is the message of Greg Pierce's book *The Mass Is Never Ended*, discussed in the chapter "In Their Own Words." A sample sermon and some hymns from both the Episcopal and Lutheran hymnals are referenced in appendix B: Getting in Shape, with more found at www.RadicalSending.com.

- Maintain a focus on the last part of the liturgy: the postcommunion prayer of "Send us now into the world . . ." and the Dismissal [an expanded version]: "Let us go forth into our worlds of work, school, community, and family rejoicing in the power of the Spirit." After receiving the bread of life and the cup of salvation, our food for the journey, the most important part of worship is our marching orders—to hit the doors—to *go*! What would a congregation's community life look like if its mission statement was, "We prepare people for the Dismissal"?

- Have laypeople preach on their personal sense of ministry in daily life. Their stories can speak powerfully to the congregation. Even more powerful, in many congregations, will be the clergy leader yielding the pulpit to a member of the congregation. Several lay sermons can be found at www.RadicalSending.com.

- Use the Prayers of the People to offer up a different daily life activity of members of the congregation over a period of Sundays. You can begin with a cycle built around major vocational areas—for instance, education, law enforcement, home making, health care, construction, or energy production—and publicize your desire to add others as requested. See appendices B: Getting in Shape and E: Strength for the Journey for possibilities as well as www.RadicalSending.com.

- Gather a group to write Prayers of the People for a season, focusing on the congregation's calling to be a base camp sustaining people's daily lives. Such a ministry focus is particularly appropriate during Epiphany or immediately after Pentecost. One such group took care to incorporate themes, words, and phrases drawn from the lectionary for the season.

- Invite members of the congregation to submit vocation-specific prayers. Such prayers could be the product of a group that shares a particular workplace or profession.

- Expand your repertoire of prayers used with some regularity in worship (since repetition is a powerful teacher that equips us to "pray by heart"). In *The Mass Is Never Ended*, Greg Pierce offers two that are particularly powerful: "The Litany of Work" by David and Angela Kaufmann and a Eucharistic prayer by Edward Schillebeeckx.[177]

- Make creative use of Labor Day and/or Rogation Sunday (The Sixth Sunday of Easter). One congregation adopted the custom on Labor Day Sunday of asking worshippers to come in their workday clothes—the surgeon in scrubs, the rancher in jeans, the cook in chef's toque and uniform. Another asked worshippers to choose a symbol of their daily work to bring to the altar for a blessing—backpacks for students, law books for lawyers, computers for administrative assistants and reporters. See appendices B: Getting in Shape and D: Messages from the Trail for possibilities.

- Designate a particular week or season for sharing stories. One congregation at its daily Eucharist during the first week of Easter asked laypeople to speak about their "witness" to the Resurrection in their daily lives.

- Commission persons in their daily life. Used on an occasional basis, it's eye-opening for the congregation to participate in acknowledging and blessing the work done beyond the church grounds. Recognizing a group of members who extend the congregation's message into the community affirms the impact one congregation can have. See appendix B: Getting in Shape for examples.

Reimagined Pastoral Care

It's easy to think of pastoral care primarily as helping those in physical or emotional or spiritual need. Certainly that's important; but what if we broadened its reach to include supporting and affirming people in the places of their strengths—on the job, in the home, at the school, in the community? These strategies are especially effective when clergy takes the lead, embodying the congregation's ability to look outside the church walls.

- Inspire your clergy leaders to make visits to members of the congregation in their workplaces, asking the key questions: What do you do here? What is the Sunday-Monday, the faith connection, with what you do here? (Most will hesitate on this, which becomes the "teachable moment" to explore the gifts and talents that they bring to their work as God-given.) What challenges do you encounter? How does your faith sustain you in dealing with those challenges? Who/what influenced you in making your faith connection? What could/does your congregation do to support you in your ministry? Get a business card from the visit. (See Fletcher's story in the introduction and the stories in chapters "In Their Own Words," "Sending Congregations," "Servants in Daily Life," and "Making the Transitions" as well as appendix C: Field Trips for more about workplace visits, as well as at www. RadicalSending.com.)

- Create marketplace lunches, inviting people to take a few moments during their workday to consider how their faith and their work intersect. Some of the Christian formation ideas above could provide discussion starters.

- Create a bulletin board designated to recognize your congregation's ministry in daily life. Possible uses include displaying business cards from visits and lunches, photos of members in their workplaces, articles mentioning their workplace activities, and other postings.

- When a member is recognized, honored, promoted, and so on in nonchurch efforts, send a congratulatory note, publish the news via the congregation's media platforms, or post a newspaper or workplace article about the honor on your bulletin board.

- Develop and train a team of pastoral visitors who routinely engage members of the congregation in conversations about their daily lives and how their faith informs what they do.

Multiplatform Communication

Because of the many different platforms for communication available to congregations, it's essential to make use of social media along with the congregation's website, worship bulletins, bulletin boards, and newsletters to promote the vision.

- Post, preferably at the entrance of the church building, a collage of pictures of members of the congregation engaged in the activities of their daily life. Remember to include all ages.

- Use quotes about base camp culture and ministry in daily life in bulletins, newsletters, bulletin boards, outdoor signs, and anywhere else you can think of. See appendix D: Messages from the Trail for quotes as well as www.RadicalSending.com.

- Publish articles in your congregation's newsletters written by members, sharing how they live out their ministries in their world. See the chapter "Servants in Daily Life" for examples.

- Create a social media or YouTube channel for conversation, interviews, and testimony about ministry in daily life.

- Create a Radical Sending bulletin board to post information on the radically sending team.

Signs of Hope: Questions and Friendly Experiments

These expressions of the congregation's gathered life—formation, liturgy, pastoral care, and communication—cross-pollinate as they function together. They raise awareness of each person's daily life ministry and help the congregation claim its ministry as a radically sending base camp, supporting the members on their life journeys. The desired effect is to inspire the members of our faith communities to ask key questions: "As people of faith—at work, in our community, in our home, in our relationships—how do we partner with God to realize the kingdom of God, right where we are? How can we live the gospel in such a way that we welcome the kingdom of God wherever we show up?"[178]

Remember Jack Fortin's comment:

I do see signs of hope. It's not a question of those who "get it." It's a much more humble approach. . . . We need models of hope, what I call "friendly experiments." . . . The key is to engage in friendly experiments, and recognize that we're all trying to figure it out. There is no one formula. . . . It's walking, and then talking about it.[179]

You are that sign of hope. Your "friendly experiments" are valuable. In this book we have been sharing our passion and offering some of the friendly experiments that we have found helpful. Your experience is an indigenous one, and we need you to share it as you journey along. Please be sure to share your insights and experiences on our website, www.RadicalSending.com, so we can all learn and grow together.

Nurturing the Base Camp: Habits to Cultivate

In all you do, keep in mind that incorporating change means being intentional about combating the force of homeostasis. The process of making "radical sending" a part of your congregation's life together is a marathon, not a sprint. Your core small group will need to work as a team, and to encourage one another along the way. You will need to keep coming back to the group and to practices that work for you and for your congregation. Keep studying key Scripture texts and, we hope, this book. And, in addition, help your core group employ tactics for affirming, and where necessary, incorporating these habits in your congregation's corporate life:

Deep Listening

Cultivate the habit of "listening with the ear of your heart," as Benedict urged in his rule for monastic communities. Practice hearing beyond the words to the gift that the speaker is offering. Remember the power of silence in encouraging wisdom and creativity to emerge.

Opportunities for Agency

Provide times and places where members of the congregation are empowered to exercise leadership, make decisions, and take responsibility. The recognition that "I am the agent of my own life" is the mark of mature self-actualization. When the members of a congregation "exercise agency," they are taking responsibility for their life together as a faith community. This means both creating occasions for success and making your congregation a safe place to fail, as long as learning takes place. Entrepreneurs and change agents know they cannot move so cautiously that failure is not an option. In building a new culture, leaders build synergy by taking measured risks, failing fast, and incorporating lessons learned.

Campfires

Intentionally make space for times and places where hikers are encouraged to bring stories back from their treks. These opportunities for sharing need to be so safe that incomplete and unsuccessful stories stimulate as much interest and learning as the stories of transformation. Not only do the storytellers practice sharing the Good News of God at work in their lives; the hearers become increasingly skillful at listening with open hearts, so that they perceive signs of God acting in places the teller might not even be aware of.

Team Building

Offer occasions for reshaping interactions among group members so that the gifts of every member are valued and celebrated. For some, this will be a change from top-down or Lone Ranger functioning. For others, it will bring a realization that in the base camp, there are partners to be found who can offer missing skills or fresh insights. And for still others, the congregation will begin to resemble their strength-leveraging workplace, where team-based function is the norm.

Affirmation of Current Ministries that Further a Base Camp Ethos

Recognize those elements already in place in the life of the congregation that support—or might be reshaped to encourage—the congregation in its functioning as a radically sending base camp. This practice also leads to noticing ministries or efforts that rob energy from the congregation's growing base camp focus.

Frequent Celebrations

Acknowledge and rejoice together when milestones are achieved, anniversaries remembered, dreams realized, and tasks accomplished. Celebration is a key element of community, which is defined more by relationship than by tasks. Recognizing progress or achievements doesn't have to be elaborate. The key elements are setting aside time to: (1) acknowledge the hard work and God's grace that have brought the congregation to a new vision, (2) look back at the distance travelled and the old that has been left behind, and (3) rejoice at God's call to keep moving. Parties, photos, recognition in worship, news articles, tokens of appreciation, commissioning liturgies, congratulatory letters, even a pause for thanksgiving can fit the bill. Renewed energy and commitment are the pay-off.

These habits of community life nurture healthy base camp culture. Making them a part of the congregation's ongoing life will equip your congregation to practice radical sending, will sustain hikers when they leave the base camp, and will draw those hikers back to the community, bearing their stories of faith at work, in their own lives and in the lives of others.

GOING FORTH

1. *For noticing or sharing with others:* What idea or thought in this chapter caught your imagination, surprised you, challenged your assumptions, inspired you, raised a question, gave you hope, cautioned you, or opened a new perspective? How does that insight relate to your life as a sent Christian?

2. *For analysis:* Where are you seeing the base camp vision take root—formation, liturgy, pastoral care, communication, elsewhere?

3. *For reflection:* Who in the congregation is flourishing or bearing fruit? Who needs to be heard more fully? Who is shepherding those flocks?

4. *For discussion or discernment:* Where do you see signs of hope? What "friendly experiments" are you celebrating? How can you build on what you're learning?

5. *For action:* Review your congregation's organizational structure to see how it can help support your "sending" culture.

Conclusion: Encouragement on the Journey

Jesus is in the Legislature where I am called to serve.
If he were not there, I should not be there either.

THE HONORABLE BYRON RUSHING, MEMBER OF THE MASSACHUSETTS LEGISLATURE
AND VICE PRESIDENT, HOUSE OF DEPUTIES OF THE EPISCOPAL CHURCH

The first demand on a carpenter's religion is that
he should make good tables. What use is anything
else if in the very center of his life and occupation
he is insulting God with bad carpentry?

DOROTHY SAYERS (*WHY WORK?* 1942)

We conclude where we began, with a call for a new paradigm in the local congregation's way of doing business: to move from an institution-centered to a radical sending–centered vision. At the heart of this change is the local congregation. It is the base camp; the place of encouraging, nurturing, equipping, and affirming the calling of the hikers in their daily lives of home, and work, and school, and community, and leisure. It is the place for "the apostles' teaching and fellowship, the breaking of bread, and the prayers." It is the launch pad for the rocket, the gas station for the car, the harbor for the fishing boat, the huddle before the next play, the timeout to restrategize. It is the important and necessary way station on the journey. But it is not the destination. The destination is the world of Christians' everyday lives. It calls both for the congregation to take seriously the daily lives of its members and for the members to see that it is in their daily lives that they live out their baptismal faith.

As you may have noticed, we have not focused on congregational outreach, as important as that might be. We have focused on what the plumber does with his plumbing, what the nurse does with his nursing, what the teenager does with his dating, what the coach does with her coaching, what the banker does when she goes home, what the citizen does in the voting booth—in short, whatever we as Christians do in whatever makes up our daily lives. All of that is important to God, and the good news is that wherever we are, God is already there. Our job is to join God in those places, living out God's mission.

We are not proposing some new "program." As first-century catechumens would tell us, taking on Christ is to connect one's faith to every aspect of one's life. As our Lutheran brothers and sisters remind us, it was part of the Reformation fervor—and it has yet to be realized. More than sixty years have passed since the 1954 Assembly of the World Council of Churches stated:

> The real battles of faith today are being fought in factories, shops, offices, and farms, in political parties and government agencies, in countless homes, in the press, radio and television, in the relationship of nations. Very often it is said the Church should "go into these spheres," but the fact is that the Church *is* already in these spheres in the persons of its laity.[180]

A Reality Check and a Dream

In light of this, a reality check: Isn't Christ the Lord of our daily lives as much as the Lord of our church's programs? If so, how might a congregation embrace a paradigm that includes the places beyond the church doors where the hikers "live and move and have their being"?

In short, how could a congregation's life be seen as a staging area, not the destination, for its members on their daily hikes, the place of replenishment providing spiritual nurture? Then the Dismissal truly becomes the marching orders of the baptized. And our daily lives, lived largely outside the walls of the church, can be understood as a holy endeavor:

> It is a gross error to suppose that the Christian cause goes forward solely or chiefly on weekends. What happens on the regular weekdays may be far more important, so far as the Christian faith is concerned than what happens on Sunday. . . . The idea is that God can call us to many kinds of activity and that secular work well done is a holy enterprise.[181]

In order to live into this radical sending image, a congregation would consider how it encourages, nurtures, equips, and affirms the baptized in their daily lives. It could explore how it links people of faith in support groups either by profession or by geography. It could provide forums where people are able to discern not only where their talents and gifts are but where their passions and their hearts are, where they are able to process how their faith connects with their daily lives. The importance of visits to the places where people work and live could be realized. Liturgically, the congregation could provide opportunities for affirmation of people in their work, just as it does in commissioning people in their church-related activities. It could provide regular weekly prayers for people in the marketplaces of life. The congregation's newsletters and communication platforms could become a source of stories of how members connect their faith with their everyday life.

A congregation would be the supply depot for the hikers with whatever they might need in terms of encouragement, nourishment, equipment, and affirmation for the weekly journey out from the camp onto the mountain. The ordained become, as one among the baptized, the persons called to lead in supporting the hikers in their journey.

What could be more exciting—or more true to the gospel? As Jesus sent out the seventy disciples and told the apostles to "Go," so we are sent forth from the congregation in the name of Christ to go into our worlds to be the Christ in all that we are and all that we do. Remember the reaction of the seventy when they returned from their mission of sharing the Good News? They were overjoyed, astounded, and jubilant to share with one another the responses of the people and the demons they encountered on the road. Imagine that energy among the people of your congregation, when they too have the opportunity to share with one another the stories of their faith at work.

We have that legacy. It is in our Christian DNA to see in all aspects of our lives the ministerial calling embedded in the Baptismal Covenant. Our prayer is that we, the people of God, might claim it and demand that our congregations encourage, nurture, equip, and affirm us as we live into it.

Greg Pierce offers a hopeful story:

A Story about God at Work

A woman went into a marketplace, looked around, and saw a sign that read, "God's Fruit Market."

"Thank goodness, it's about time," the woman said to herself.

She went inside and said, "I would like a perfect banana, a perfect cantaloupe, a perfect strawberry, and a perfect peach."

God, who was behind the counter, shrugged and said, "I'm sorry, Madam, I sell only seeds."[182]

So be bold, joining God in planting seeds. Remember Christ's assurance, "The one who believes in me will also do the works that I do and, in fact, will do greater works than these" (John 14:12). And remember, in this post-Christendom world of the twenty-first century, belonging and behaving pave the way for believing.

We want to thank you for your openness to our passion. We are grateful for your willingness to move your congregation toward adopting and adapting the practices of radical sending. We want to cheer you on as you embrace base camp culture as your congregation's way of sustaining one another on your journey in the Way of Jesus.

And in all the work we do, may we rejoice in God's presence on the journey with us:

> For our work that sheds light on the darkness,
> *We praise you, God.*

> For our work that creates order from chaos,
> *We praise you, God.*

> For our work that builds peace out of hostility,
> *We praise you, God.*

> For our work that helps others,
> *We praise you, God.*

> For our work that serves others,
> *We praise you, God.*

For our work that empowers others,
We praise you, God.

For our work that inspires others,
We praise you, God.

For our work that enriches and ennobles all creation,
We praise you, God.[183]

Gratitudes

As authors, we are in the debt of many who have paved the way for us. Chief among these is Steve Jacobsen, the creator of the base camp metaphor, which has been the wellspring of this book. Stephanie Spellers, author of *Radical Welcome*, laid a foundation for our work that shaped much of what we have done.

We also owe special thanks to each of the "hikers" who have contributed their stories—of their own walks and of their congregations' efforts. Their insights and their experiences have put flesh on the bones of this work, and have grounded our observations in the authenticity of lived faith in daily life.

In deepening our knowledge of the riches of Celtic spirituality, we are indebted to Mary Earle of San Antonio, Texas; John Phillip Newell of Edinburgh, Scotland; and Mark White, Susan Wilkes, and Margie Nea of Richmond, Virginia.

We were enabled to hear the voices of our Lutheran friends through Richard Bruesehoff, Dwight DuBois, Jack Fortin, Gregory Kaufman, and Craig Nessan, who provided energizing conversations, writings, and referrals as well as many suggestions of ways to incorporate the Lutheran Ministry in Daily Life tradition. Similarly, we learned much from our Mennonite friends, especially Keith Graber Miller whose paper, *Transforming Vocation: A Mennonite Perspective*, provided a core resource, and Ryan Ahlgrim, First Mennonite Church, Richmond,

Virginia, whose thoughtful e-mails and considerable knowledge connected us significantly to important sources.

A special thanks goes to Blair Bigelow, Bruce Cruser, Dick Ritsch, and Tom Smith of the St. Paul's, Richmond, Marketplace Values group for their time and energy in discerning Christian workplace values; to the Honorable Bill Mims, Virginia State Supreme Court Justice, for sharing his advice and his excellent servant leadership PowerPoint; and to Wilson Whitehurst, the paving contractor whose initial quote set the stage for succeeding personal stories.

Through the entire writing process, the insights and forbearance of our editor, Sharon Ely Pearson of Church Publishing, assured that this book would become a reality. Copy editor Amy Wagner's eagle eyes and diligent research have enhanced our accuracy and our credibility. We are grateful.

Thanks be to God for each of these "Good News bearers," sent into the world to share the light of Christ with everyone they encounter in their daily lives. And above all, thanks be to God for sending us all on the journey, in Christ's name.

✝ Appendices

Practicing for the Climb

Engaging Christian Formation

A. Ministry of the Baptized in Daily Life: The Congregation as a Base Camp

A Retreat or Intensive Study

This format has a number of possible uses. It can be a series of educational events over six sessions, one theme per session; or one session by having six small groups, each dealing with one of the themes; or some other combination such as a retreat or intensive study format. Below is an outline of the Leader's Guide, with the full process detailed at www.RadicalSending.com.

Introduction to the Process

Small Group Themes for Conversation

1. **Vocation**
   - *Read* (suggested quote)
   - *Questions for Discussion*

2. **Bible Study**
   - *Read* (suggested biblical passages)
   - *Questions for Discussion*

3. **A Day in Your Life**
   - *Journal*
   - *Questions for Discussion*

4. **Your Work and Ministry**
   - *Read* (suggested quotes)
   - *Questions for Discussion*

5. **Radical Sending in the Book of Common Prayer**
   - *Read* (Book of Common Prayer selections)
   - *Questions for Discussion*

6. **Your Work and Faith**
   - *Read* (quotes)
   - *Questions for Discussion*

Large Group Plenary Discussion

Closing Prayer

B. A Critical Incident Format for a Faith at Work Discussion

This Critical Incident Format comes from the Education for Ministry program developed at the School of Theology, University of the South, Sewanee, Tennessee.° What follows is an adaptation that can be used as a small group format. One congregation used this with groups of four to five persons over their lunch hour, meeting weekly or every other week; *the group vows to keep the conversation confidential.* There was a rotation of who was "critical," which could be preempted if another participant had an immediately critical issue. The purpose was not to solve the problem, but rather to get some perspective on it from a Christian viewpoint.

Format:

- An individual presents a problem, situation, or event that comes from his or her own experience. The group helps the presenter isolate the most critical issue. The presenter then makes a one-sentence statement of that issue. (This process helps to succinctly identify what the real issue is, which sometimes is different from what the presenter originally indicated.)

- Each member in the group "owns" the issue presented by sharing a problem, situation, or event from his or her life of a similar nature.

- The group examines the issue, exploring together biblical events and contemporary cultural dynamics that bear similarities, checking their reality against the critical incident.

° http://efm.sewanee.edu.

- The group explores options available and possible courses of action, but not to resolve the issue.
- The group shares their learnings.
- Prayer is passed from person to person about the issue and other concerns.

C. PowerPoint Presentations

Three PowerPoint presentations: "Baptism and Radical Sending," "The Base Camp and Radical Sending," and "The Eucharist and Radical Sending" are available for download on the website www.Radical Sending.com.

Additional Christian formation resources may be found at www.RadicalSending.com.

Getting in Shape

Resources for
Transformational Liturgy

Sermons

Sermons provide an opportunity to connect the gospel with our practices today of living out our baptismal promises in the world of daily life. Examples include Fletcher's sermon, "Peter Goes Fishing: Where Sunday Meets Monday" and Philip A. Brooks's (a layperson from Richmond, VA) sermon about recognizing his vocation as one of craftsman as opposed to career. Both serve as examples of how to make the connection with faith at work and can be read at www. RadicalSending.com.

Hymnody

The words we sing in our hymns can lift up the ministry of all the baptized during our worship. Every denominational hymnal contains numerous hymns the focus on "ministry," including:

The Hymnal 1982[†]

312 Strengthen for service . . .
340 For the bread . . .
347 Go forth for God . . .
602 Jesu, Jesu . . .

Wonder, Love and Praise[‡]

778 We all are one in mission
780 Lord, you give the great commission

[†] *The Hymnal 1982* (New York: Church Pension Fund, 1985).

[‡] *Wonder, Love, and Praise: A Supplement to The Hymnal 1982* (New York: Church Pension Fund, 1997).

Lutheran Book of Worship[§]

543 Go, my children . . .
659 Will you let me be your servant . . .
679 For the fruit . . .
722 O Christ, your heart . . .

With One Voice[¶]

753 You are the seed . . .

Rogation Sunday (The Sixth Sunday of Easter)

Celebrating Our Ministries in Daily Life

Rogation (Latin, *to ask*) began in rural and fishing communities *asking* God's blessing of their means of production, such as seeds and soil, boats and bait. In reclaiming this day in our more modern industrial and service economy, the focus on the means of production remains the same, but the symbols shift to whatever *occupies* our daily lives: our jobs, our volunteer efforts, our recreation, our family life, and so on. On Rogation Sunday, invite all to *ask* God's blessing in three ways:

1. Through offering a small symbol of one's daily life and work, such as a business card, a cell phone, a day timer, a ticker tape, a lesson plan, a homework sheet, or a cooking spoon, to be placed in an alms basket and made part of the offertory (to be returned after the service).

2. Through a liturgy affirming each of us in our daily "occupations." This is another means of continuing our role as a base camp supporting, affirming, and encouraging each of us in all that we are and do.

3. Through a litany focused on the various vocations upon which our lives depend.

Further liturgy resources may be found in appendix E: Strength for the Journey and at www.RadicalSending.com.

---

§ *Lutheran Book of Worship* (Minneapolis: Augsburg Fortress, 2006).
¶ *With One Voice* (Minneapolis: Augsburg Fortress, 1995).

Field Trips
Reimagined Pastoral Care

Marketplace Visits

A way for clergy to enter significantly into the daily life of Christians is by visiting them where they spend much of their working hours on the job. That may be in a factory, at home, in an office—wherever the people of God are engaged in their work. A model found to be meaningful to both clergy and parishioners is "the marketplace visit." In one congregation the rector arranges visits during the workday as parishioners' schedules allow. In another, the rector sets aside most Thursdays, scheduling lunches on a one-on-one basis with members of the congregation. That format is simple: Each brings his or her own brown bag and they met across the parishioner's desk or its equivalent. The importance of being a presence at the workplace provides an affirmation that cannot be achieved in any other way. This has had a salutatory effect on parishioners' sense of call and ministry.

For most, it may be the first time these kinds of questions have been asked. If so, it becomes a teachable moment to explore what God-given talents the parishioner brings to his or her job. Using words like "calling," "vocation," and "ministry" can take on new meaning for the individual.

The conversations center on these questions:

- What do you do here?
- What connection do you experience between Sunday and Monday, the connection with your faith?
- If the person has a sense of ministry at work, then ask: Who or what influenced you?
- If the person hesitates (most will), this becomes the "teachable moment" to explore the gifts and talents that they bring to their work as God-given.

- What could/does your congregation and its leadership do to support, affirm, you in your ministry?
- Two other possible questions: What challenges do you encounter? How does/could your faith sustain you in dealing with those challenges?
- Conclude with a prayer offering the person's ministry to God.
- Get a business card from the visit.

It is important to share the questions with those to be visited beforehand. The results vary depending upon the person; for some it can be a learning experience as this may be the first time they have considered the connection; for some it is an affirmation of their calling and ministry; for some it can be a challenge to struggle with a sense of ministry where they are; for some it can be an "aha," when they realize that they do have a calling, a ministry. It is important to recognize that there can be a distinction between a real sense of call: "God has put me in this place" and a sense of ministry: "In this place I can live into the Baptismal Covenant to 'seek and serve, . . . respect the dignity.'" Most importantly, such visits affirm that the Church is supportive of the very work that occupies parishioners most of their working and waking hours.

An Example of a Marketplace Visit

The Rev. Dr. Sharon Wilson, Windsor Park United Church, Winnipeg, Manitoba, Canada, shares her experience with marketplace visits:

> I resolved to spend one day each month with one of my church members in their workplace. What followed has been a revelation for all of us. First we had to learn the logistics of getting me into their workplaces. I have signed more waivers and confidentiality forms than you can imagine. But all of this preparatory activity has been more than compensated by the insight gained. I have spent time with a security guard, an elementary school vice-principal, the director of a residential facility for troubled teens, a programmer for a religious broadcasting network, a special education teacher, a speech language pathologist, a federal civil servant, and a medical laboratory technologist. I've witnessed someone break up fights and another extract DNA. I have been moved by the skills and dedication of these folk to the work they do. I have listened as I heard of the stresses and strains

faced in the workplace and at home as the two spheres of life connect and collide. Greg Pierce held before me the challenge to minister to the guy in the tollbooth on the I-94. Nothing could have been more powerful or energizing.

Her conversations moved in this way:

- What do you like about your job?
- Do you feel like you're making a difference?
- Are there times when you feel your values are challenged?
- In what ways do you see your work as part of your effort to live faithfully?
- What are the stresses or frustrations at work?
- If you could choose the sermon topic one Sunday, what would it be?

Messages from the Trail

Resources for Communication

Whether you use your Sunday worship bulletin, church website, or any social media platform, any of the following can be used to help keep your message of "radical sending" in the hearts and minds of your congregation. The quotes below span time and place in Christian history. They have multiple uses: as "one-liners" for bulletins and/or newsletters, enlarged as posters, quick discussion starters for education events ("How does this statement relate to you in your daily life as a Christian?"), or relevant quotations for talks and presentations. For more quotes, visit www.RadicalSending.com.

"We have got our weekdays separated from our Sundays and our work separated from our worship, with the inevitable result that our work has become bitter and our worship has become empty." —George Macleod of Iona"

❋ ❋ ❋

"To pray is to work and to work is to pray." —Benedictine Rule

❋ ❋ ❋

"The action of the Eucharist is never completed in the church (building). It always finds its completion as we take it outside, into the world." —Miles Yates, former chaplain, General Theological Seminary, New York City

---

"" Unless otherwise noted, from Linda L. Grenz and J. Fletcher Lowe, eds., *Ministry in Daily Life: A Guide to Living the Baptismal Covenant* (New York: Domestic and Foreign Missionary Society, 1996), http://arc.episcopalchurch.org/ministry/daily.htm (accessed April 20, 2015).

❊ ❊ ❊

"If I believe that there is a loving God, who has created me and wants me to be part of a people who will carry the good news of the love of that God to the world, what difference does that make when I go to my office at nine o'clock Monday morning? What difference does it make in my office that I believe there is a loving God, that God loves me, and that God loves all human beings exactly as that God loves me? What different kinds of decisions do I make? What am I called to do in that office?" —Verna Dozier, *The Authority of the Laity* (Washington, DC: Alban Institute, 1982), 16.

❊ ❊ ❊

"Hands to work. Hearts to God." —Amish

❊ ❊ ❊

"Authentic Christianity is designed for the home and the community, the office and the shop, the club and the campus, the market, factory and farm. Christianity is for everyday, wherever one is under whatever circumstances. Christianity is for between Sundays!" —U.S. Senate Chaplain Richard C. Halverson, *Walk with God Between Sundays* (Grand Rapids: Zondervan, 1965)

❊ ❊ ❊

"Ministry in the world is you and me, you and me, following Jesus, and working for the reconciliation of the world to God, everywhere we are. In our families, in our vocations, but especially in our workplaces." — The Honorable Bryon Rushing, keynote address, National Episcopal Evangelism Leadership Conference, November 30, 1992.

❊ ❊ ❊

"Genesis says that humans were created in the image of God, so all of our work—not just church work—is holy. We are called to be co-creators, with God, of a flourishing life on Earth. 'It is really a profound act of engaging the kingdom of God.'" —Dave Evans, cofounder of the videogame giant Electronic Arts and a design professor at Stanford, quoted in Rob Moll, "Doing God's Work: At the Office" *The Wall Street Journal*, February 20, 2011.

❀ ❀ ❀

"To believe in one's own priesthood is to see the extraordinary dimensions of an ordinary life, to see the hand of God at work in the world and to see one's own hands as necessary to that work. Whether those hands are diapering an infant, assembling an automobile or balancing a corporate account, they are God's hands, claimed by God at baptism for the accomplishment of God's will on earth." —Barbara Brown Taylor, *The Preaching Life* (Lanham, MD: Rowman & Littlefield, 1993), 32.

❀ ❀ ❀

"We are called to let our light so shine not just in the context of the four walls of the church but out in the community as well." —Sue Mallory, *LayNet* (Summer 2003): 4.

❀ ❀ ❀

"What does my work have to do with religion?

"Well, we choose how we look at the world and at life. You're a taxi driver. But you are also a piece of the tissue that connects all humanity. You're taking me to the airport. I'll go to a different city and give a couple of lectures that might touch or help or change someone. I couldn't have gotten there without you. You help make that connection happen. I heard on your two-way radio that after you drop me off, you're going to pick up a woman from the hospital and take her home. That means that you'll be the first non-medical person she encounters after being in a hospital. You will be a small part of her healing process, an agent in her re-entry into the world of health. You may then pick up someone from the train station who has come home from seeing a dying parent. You may take someone to the house of the one that he or she will ask to join in marriage. You're a connector, a bridge builder. You're one of the unseen people who make the world work as well as it does. That is holy work. You may not think of it this way, but yours is a sacred mission." —Rabbi Jeffrey K. Salkin, *Being God's Partner* (Woodstock, VT: Jewish Lights), 170.

Strength for the Journey

Prayers

Additional prayers touching on many aspects of daily life are available at www.RadicalSending.com.

A Weekly Prayer Cycle: The Baptized in Their Daily Life and Work

Below is a sampling of a series of petitions for the baptized in the places where they work. As with other cycles, this weekly petition will be offering up a different workplace ministry, such as health care, environmental, or social service. To access the petitions for a full-year cycle, please visit www.RadicalSending.com.

We pray for all the baptized in their daily work, especially those of our congregation and community who are:

January—Week 1: In the legal profession, including lawyers, paralegals, and their support staff.

January—Week 2: In the arts, including painters, sculptors, and designers.

February—Week 3: In retail, including managers, clerks, and promotional staff.

April—Week 2: On highway and road construction, including contractors, equipment operators, work crews, and maintenance crews.

May—Week 1: In the hotel and motel industry, including managers, receptionists, concierges, housekeeping staff, and auxiliary personnel.

June—Week 3: In museums and galleries, including curators, artists, docents, educators, and support staff.

August—Week 3: In the automotive industry, including designers, manufacturers, salespersons, insurers, repair persons, and office support staff.

October—Week 1: In the pet business, including veterinarians, breeders, kennel workers, managers, and salespersons.

November—Week 4: In the garbage, trash, sewage, and recycling business, including collectors, treatment, and land fill personnel.

A Liturgy of Commitment for People in Their Daily Life[tt]

Celebrant: My Brothers and Sisters in Christ Jesus: we are all baptized by one Spirit into one Body, and given gifts for a variety of ministries for the common good. You have come forward today to ask God's blessings on the particular work that you do. Please now name the occupation for which you seek God's blessing.

Response: (Each person names his or her occupation.)

Celebrant: In the ministry of your daily life and work, will you proclaim by word and example the Good News of God in Christ?

Response: I will, with God's help.

Celebrant: In your daily occupation, will you seek and serve Christ in all persons, loving your neighbor as yourself?

Response: I will, with God's help.

Celebrant: In the vocation to which God has called you, will you strive for justice and peace among all people, and respect the dignity of every human being?

Response: I will, with God's help.

Celebrant: Let us pray. Almighty God, whose Son Jesus Christ in his earthly life shared our toil and hallowed our labor: be present with your people where they work. Deliver us from the service of self alone, and grant that we, remembering the account that we must one day give, may be faithful stewards of your good gifts; for the sake of him who came among us as one who serves, your Son our Savior Jesus Christ. *Amen.*

---

†† Developed by Fletcher Lowe, originally published in Linda L. Grenz and J. Fletcher Lowe Jr., eds., *Ministry in Daily Life: A Guide to Living the Baptismal Covenant* (New York: Domestic and Foreign Missionary Society, 1996), 140–41.

In the Name of God and of this congregation, I recognize and affirm your commitment to follow Christ in the vocation to which God has called you. May the Holy Spirit guide and strengthen you to bear faithful witness to Christ, and to carry on his work of reconciliation in the world. *Amen.*

Litany for the Ministry of All the Baptized[‡‡]

Officiant: Let us thank God for those persons who have responded to Christ's call to serve him in the world.

People: Lord, we know that you call us to serve our neighbor in love in the world in which we live.

Officiant: For those who seek both to glorify you and to help their neighbor through their work.

People: We give you thanks, O Lord. (R—*response to be repeated after each petition*)

Officiant: For those who are actively involved in the political process of our community, state, and nation. *(R)*

Officiant: For those who work for social justice, fair housing, and equal opportunity for both sexes and all races. *(R)*

Officiant: For those who work to make our community a safe and pleasant place to live—engineers, bakers, contractors, architects, fire and police personnel. *(R)*

Officiant: For those who serve as homemakers, providing care, nourishment, and a secure haven for families. *(R)*

Officiant: For those who teach and care for our children, both salaried staff and volunteer aides. *(R)*

Officiant: For those who serve in the armed services, especially those in harm's way. *(R)*

Officiant: For those who minister to the sick as medical professionals, as visitors or volunteers. *(R)*

Officiant: For those who visit the lonely and the shut-in, and for those who find time to listen to the troubled and distressed. *(R)*

Officiant: For those who serve the hungry, the homeless, and the unemployed. *(R)*

Officiant: For all those whose labor and effort are unseen and unsung, but who carry Christ's ministry in the world. *(R)*

[‡‡] Adapted for this book and originally developed by Fletcher Lowe as "Litany for the Ministry of the Laity," in *Ministry in Daily Life: A Guide to Living the Baptismal Covenant* (New York: Domestic and Foreign Missionary Society, 1996), 153–54.

Officiant: Let us thank God for the love we have experienced in Christ Jesus, who motivates and empowers us to serve others in his name.

People: O Lord, we recall the words of your Son when he said, "I came not to be served, but to serve." He saw our needs and he ministered to us in love. We thank you for calling us to follow in his footsteps. We ask you to work through us, and help us always to work for you. Keep our eyes open to the possibilities around us; grant us strength and courage to serve the Christ in others. In Christ's name we pray. Amen.

Examples of Daily Life Prayers

For Vocation in Daily Work

Almighty God our heavenly Father, you declare your glory and show forth your handiwork in the heavens and in the earth: Deliver us in our various occupations from the service of self alone, that we may do the work you give us to do in truth and beauty and for the common good; for the sake of him who came among us as one who serves, your Son Jesus Christ our Lord, who lives and reigns with you and the Holy Spirit, one, God, for ever and ever. Amen. (BCP, 261)

Prayer for Managers

Our God, Creator of Heaven and Earth. Thank you for the opportunity to be of service to you and a blessing to those in our employ. Create in us a mind and heart to honor each employee that you place in our care, as you have honored us. Help us to remember that all opinions are valuable and every position no matter what the responsibility is essential for the successful operation of the organization. Teach us to be kind and fair. Help make this working environment one that is pleasant; where each employee knows he/she is valued and their talents and gifts are appreciated. Be with us in our decision-making and bless us we pray, in Jesus' name. Amen. §§

When You're a Customer

Give us eyes, O God, to see the worker in the work. Not just the title or the salary scale. Not just the output and the product. Let us really see you serve us lunch in the diner, when you give us insurance forms to complete, when you take our money at the tollbooth, Let us see you in one another. Amen.¶¶

---

§§ *Prayers for the Workplace* (King of Prussia, PA: American Baptist Home Mission Societies). Their pamphlet with other workplace prayers is available at www.radical sending.com.

¶¶ Donna Schaper, *Celebrate Labor Day* (Liguori, MO: Liguori Publications, 1997).

Signposts
Websites and Organizations

After Sunday offers resources that cover the main areas of vocation, reflective living, discipleship, and work (in addition to a set of resources focused on the essence of "After Sunday" thinking). Each set of resources is made up of between six and eight sessions and is free to download. www.aftersunday.org.uk

Celebrate Your Work focuses on the work we do on a daily basis as something to be celebrated, not endured. http://celebrateyourwork.com

Episcopalians on Baptismal Mission serves as an advocate and a resource for furthering all Christians in living out their baptismal promises in their missions and ministries in daily life within the Episcopal Church. www.livinggodsmission.org

Faith@Work is a network for sharing with each other as we strive to walk in the will of God in the workplace. Here, we can seek answers and advice, and encourage and support one another. www.faith-at-work.net

Foundations for Laity Renewal exists to serve God by creating opportunities for people to encounter God for the transformation of daily life, work, and our world. www.laityrenewal.org

The High Calling is focused on everyday conversations about work, life, and God with a broad range of articles, interviews, devotionals, videos, and inspirational stories specifically created to help integrate one's faith with work, family, and the broader culture. www.thehighcalling.org

The London Institute for Contemporary Christianity equips Christians and churches for whole-life discipleship in the world. www.licc.org.uk/

Marketplace Institute is an initiative of Regent College in Vancouver, British Columbia, that takes the gospel public by connecting faith with all of life. They provide a newsletter, a variety of conferences and articles, and a congregationally based program entitled "ReFraming" that is designed to help in radical sending. http://marketplace.regent-college.edu

Marketplace Leaders is a voice and agent to create tools that inspire, teach, and connect Christian believers to resources and relationships in order to manifest the life of Christ in their workplace call. www.marketplaceleaders.org

Member Mission is a congregationally based organization focused on "equipping the saints" for their missions in the world. www.membermission.org

Passionary: Ordinary People Making Waves is an initiative of the American Baptist Home Mission Societies in which "passionaries" are the spear point of a radical twenty-first-century mission model. They produce a weekday publication, "WORD and WITNESS," and a monthly resource, "Everyday Mission," inviting participants to "walk wet" and answer the call to discipleship, community, and justice. www.walkwet.com

Princeton Faith and Work Initiative generates intellectual frameworks and practical resources for the issues and opportunities surrounding faith and work. The Initiative investigates the ways in which the resources of various religious traditions and spiritual identities shape and inform engagement with diverse workplace issues such as ethics, values, vocation, meaning, purpose, and how people live out their faith in an increasingly pluralistic world. The Initiative explores pressing marketplace topics, including ethics, global competition and its ramifications, wealth creation and poverty, diversity and inclusion, conflicting stakeholder interests, and social responsibility. www.princeton.edu/faithandwork

Theology of Work Project offers a biblical perspective on faith and work from an independent, international organization dedicated to researching, writing, and distributing materials with a biblical perspective on non-church workplaces. www.theologyofwork.org

The Work+Shop has a mission of discipling individuals, small groups, and congregations in the life-giving ways of Jesus. The Work+Shop takes its name from the fourth chapter of the Rule of St. Benedict, a set of guidelines for the monastic life developed in the sixth century CE. By using this name, The Work+Shop is signaling its commitment to offer a way for Christian laity to become skilled in the tools of the spiritual craft in all aspects of daily life. Their offerings include a small number of weekly, biweekly, and monthly reflection groups, weekly classes in San Antonio, and online biblical studies for individuals, groups, and leadership teams. Materials are appropriate not only for people who have been Christians for a long time, but for those who are just wondering whether following Jesus might be worthwhile. http://theworkshop-sa.org

Notes from Other Hikers

Models from the Evangelical Lutheran Church of America

In recent years the Evangelical Lutheran Church of America has initiated several projects that affirm the ministry of all the baptized:

In preparation for their 2016 Churchwide Assembly, the Covenant Cluster Taskforce on Lay Theological Education circulated a model resolution for synod assemblies to consider. *The Life of Faith Initiative Model Resolution for Synod Assemblies* seeks to embody ever more fully Luther's Reformation call to the ministry of all the baptized, understanding that all the baptized share a single vocation of loving God and loving neighbors (Matt. 22:36–40) as lived out in various roles and relationships. It calls the ELCA to build upon the Life of Faith initiative with a focus on Christian vocation to "reaffirm the universal priesthood of all believers, namely, that all baptized Christians are called to minister in the name of Christ and, empowered by the Holy Spirit, to proclaim the promise of God in the world and in their various callings and to bear God's creative and redeeming Word to all the world, to meet human needs, to work for dignity and justice for all people, and peace and reconciliation among the nations."°°°

The resolution calls for the collaboration of theological education networks (including Augsburg Fortress as the denominational publisher) to promote the ministry of all the baptized and for congregations to join in this grassroots initiative in partnership for equipping individuals and congregations as learning communities at the interface of faith and life.

°°° 1993 ELCA Churchwide Assembly in response to the *Together for Ministry* report, "The Ministry of All the Baptized," 13–14; it also reflects section 7.11 of the ELCA constitution, "Ministry of the Baptized People of God."

Craig Nessan's paper "The Neighborliness (*Diakonia*) of All Believers: Toward Reimagining the Universal Priesthood" offers twenty theses that sketch out an alternative theology for the ministry of the baptized in the world under the concept "the neighborliness (*diakonia*) of all believers." In summary:

1. God sets Christian people free *from* all that holds them captive to the powers of this world and free *for* service of the neighbor in this world.

2. In baptism the Holy Spirit "ordains" every baptized person into the vocation of service to God and neighbor.

3. At the rite of affirmation of baptism, each Christian person affirms their call "to continue in the covenant God made with you in holy baptism," including proclaiming "the good news of God in Christ through word and deed, to serve all people, following the example of Jesus, and to strive for justice and peace in all the earth."

4. God employs the baptized as *the primary agents* to accomplish God's purpose of bringing life to the world.

5. "To equip the saints for the work of ministry, for building up the body of Christ" [Eph. 4:12] encompasses the ministry of evangelizing and the strategy of service to others.

6. Evangelizing begins with listening to others and taking seriously the concrete situation of those with whom we speak.

7. Shalom ministry is lived out as Christian neighborliness in the four primary arenas in which God has placed us for service to others in this world: (a) family, (b) daily work, (c) religious institutions, and (d) engagement for the common good.

8. God gives us neighbors to serve in the primary community of family in which we are located for life.

9. God gives us neighbors to serve in our daily work, no matter where that labor is lived out.

10. God gives us neighbors to serve through religious institutions as these institutions contribute to the common good.

11. God gives us neighbors to serve through engagement for the common good.

12. The rosters of the Evangelical Lutheran Church in America are each properly oriented in a theology of ministry that gives priority to equipping the baptized for neighborliness in daily life.

13. Diaconal ministers are called both to model through their own ministries and to foster among the baptized the fundamental movement from sanctuary to street, church to society, which is entailed in "the sending" from worship into the world.

14. Ordained ministers serve Word and sacrament through preaching, teaching, worship leadership, and pastoral care, in order that the baptized are set free by the Gospel of Jesus Christ *from* all that holds them captive and free *for* serving the neighbors whom God gives them in the four arenas of daily life.

15. Bishops serve the one, holy, catholic, apostolic church, so that the ministries of unity, holiness, catholicity, and apostolicity promote the neighborliness of the baptized.

16. A missional ecclesiology orients all offices of ministry toward the sending of the baptized to be the primary agents in God's mission of serving neighbors in the world.

17. Lay schools for ministry need to be guided by a missional ecclesiology that orients all offices of ministry toward *the sending of the baptized to be the primary agents in God's mission of serving neighbors in the world*.

18. Lay schools for ministry provide theological education explicitly focused on equipping and sending Christian persons to live out their baptismal vocation in the distinctive arenas of service to neighbor which are characteristic of daily life in the world.

19. A network of lay schools for ministry, linked together for mutual encouragement and the fostering of promising practices, can strengthen the church's focus on the neighborliness (*diakonia*) of all believers as the primary mission goal of the church of Jesus Christ.

20. In a network of lay schools for ministry, which foster the neighborliness of all believers, the educational programs should focus on preparing the baptized to participate in both God's right hand strategy of speaking the Gospel to others and God's left hand strategy of service to others.[†††]

Both of these documents can be read in full (and as updated) on our website: www.RadicalSending.com.

[†††] Craig L. Nessan, "The Neighborliness (*Diakonia*) of All Believers: Toward Reimagining the Universal Priesthood" (unpublished paper, Wartburg Theological Seminary, 2014). Emphasis in original.

Notes

1. David Clark, "Setting Up 'Faith at Work' Programmes," *How to Become a Creative Church Leader: A MODEM Handbook*, ed. John Nelson (London: Canterbury Press, 2008), 90.

2. *The Mass Is Never Ended* (Notre Dame, IN: Ave Maria Press, 2007).

3. From data received from Dr. C. Kirk Hadaway, Office of Congregational Research, DFMS (Domestic and Foreign Missionary Society, The Episcopal Church) (via e-mail to the authors, April 27, 2015), and Matthew Price, Vice President for Research and Data for the Church Pension Group (via e-mail to the authors, May 13, 2015).

4. Robert Banks and R. Paul Stevens, *The Complete Book of Everyday Christianity* (Downer's Grove, IL: InterVarsity Press, 1997), 159.

5. Ibid., 160–61.

6. The Right Reverend Thomas Ray, address, Diocese of Newark, January 1990.

7. Hadaway and Price data.

8. Ray, address, Diocese of Newark.

9. A. Theodore Eastman, *The Baptizing Community: Christian Initiation and the Local Congregation* (Harrisburg, PA: Morehouse Publishing, 1991), 41.

10. Ray, address, Diocese of Newark.

11. Steve Jacobsen, *Hearts to God, Hands to Work* (Herndon, VA: Alban Institute, 1997), 24.

12. Verna Dozier, *The Authority of the Laity* (Washington, DC: Alban Institute, 1984), 40.

13. Jean M. Haldane, "Ministry of Laity in Daily Life," *Action Information* (Washington, DC: Alban Institute, July/August 1989), http://oca.org/parish-ministry/theology/ministry-of-laity-in-daily-life (accessed March 31, 2015).

14. A Faith@Work article in the St. Paul's, Richmond, Virginia, monthly Epistle, September 2007.

15. St. Paul's, Richmond, Virginia, monthly Epistle, June 2005.

16. Dozier, *Authority of the Laity*, 16.

17. John H. McKenna, *Become What We Receive: A Systematic Study of the Eucharist* (Chicago/Mundelein, IL: Hillenbrand Books, 2012) and quoted by the Reverend Margaret Bullitt-Jonas in a sermon preached on August 3, 2008, www.holyhunger.com/sermons/message20080803.php#note2 (accessed March 30, 2015).

18. Teilhard de Chardin, *Hymn of the Universe* (San Francisco: Harper Collins, 1974).

19. Dr. Seuss, *Oh, The Places You'll Go!* (New York: Random House, 1990), 56.

20. David J. Bosch, *Transforming Mission: Paradigm Shifts in Theology of Mission* (Maryknoll, NY: Orbis Books, 1991), 389–90.

21. The quote, often misattributed to Carl Jung because it was inscribed over the doorway to his home, is "Vocatus atque non vocatus, deus aderit," drawn from the *Collectaneas adagiorum* of Erasmus, from http://en.wikiquote.org/wiki/Carl_Jung and http://www.creatormundi.com/product/bidden-or-not-bidden-oval-plaque/ (accessed March 17, 2015).

22. Loren Mead, *Transforming Congregations for the Future* (Bethesda, MD: Alban Institute, 1994), 41–42.

23. Dwight Zscheile, "A Missional Theology of Spiritual Formation," in *Cultivating Sent Communities: Missional Spiritual Formation*, ed. Dwight Zscheile (Grand Rapids, MI: William B. Eerdmans, 2012), 27.

24. Susan Hope, *Mission-Shaped Spirituality: The Transforming Power of Mission* (New York: Seabury Books, 2010), 2.

25. Lesslie Newbigin, *The Household of God: Lectures on the Nature of the Church* (London: SCM Press, 1953), 55.

26. www.ignatianspirituality.com/making-good-decisions/an-approach-to-good-choices/a-method-of-group-decision-making/ (accessed December 2, 2014). Adapted from William J. Byron, SJ, *Jesuit Saturdays: Sharing the Ignatian Spirit with Friends and Colleagues* (Chicago: Loyola Press, 2008).

27. www.beliefnet.com/Inspiration/2009/02/Irish-Blessings-for-Luck.aspx?p=5&b=1 (accessed March 31, 2015).

28. Matthew Fox, ed., *Western Spirituality: Historical Roots, Ecumenical Roots* (Rochester, VT: Bear and Company, 1981), 173–74.

29. David Adam, *The Edge of Glory: Prayers in the Celtic Tradition*, 8th impression (London: Triangle/SPCK, 1985/1994), 27.

30. Esther de Waal, *Every Earthly Blessing: Rediscovering the Celtic Tradition* (Harrisburg, PA: Morehouse Publishing, 1999), xv.

31. Carmichael, *Carmina Gadelica I* (Kindle edition; Santa Cruz, CA: Evinity Publishing, Inc., 2009), 231.

32. Carmichael, *Carmina Gadelica IV*, 62–63.

33. Carmichael, *Carmina Gadelica I*, 87.

34. John O'Donohue, *Eternal Echoes: Celtic Reflections on our Yearning to Belong* (New York: Harper Perenniel, 1999.)

35. John O'Donohue, *Anam Cara: A Book of Celtic Wisdom* (New York: Harper Perennial, 1998), 160–61.

36. http://www.poetry-chaikhana.com/blog/2013/08/19/john-odonohue-may-the-light-of-your-soul-guide-you/ (accessed June 20, 2015).

37. Mary Earle, "Celtic Prayer as a Way of Befriending Daily Life and Rhythms," Five Day Academy for Spiritual Formation, Camp Sumatanga, Alabama, August 7, 2014. Used with permission.

38. "As I Arise Today" is a variation of Kuno Meyer's translation of "The Deer's Cry" (The Hymn of St Patrick), http://www.beliefnet.com/Prayers/Catholic/Morning/The-Prayer-Of-St-Patrick.aspx (accessed June 20, 2015).

39. www.theemeraldisle.org (accessed March 31, 2015).

40. Keith Graber Miller, "Transforming Vocation: A Mennonite Perspective," *Mennonite Quarterly Review,* January 2009, 30. In his footnote to this passage, Graber Miller notes, "These sentences are paraphrased, in slightly different order and form, from Rupert Davies, "Vocation," in *The Westminster Dictionary of Christian Theology*, ed. Alan Richardson and John Bowden (Philadelphia, PA: Westminster Press, 1983), 601."

41. Craig L. Nessan, "The Neighborliness (*Diakonia*) of All Believers: Toward Reimagining the Universal Priesthood" (unpublished paper, Wartburg Theological Seminary, 2014), 1.

42. Richard Bruesehoff, conference call and e-mail message with authors, December 27, 2014.

43. Jack Fortin, *The Centered Life: Awakened, Called, Set Free, Nurtured* (Minneapolis: Augsburg Fortress, 2006), 94.

44. Life of Faith Initiative Model Resolution for Synod Assemblies, drafted by the Covenant Cluster Taskforce on Lay Theological Education, e-mail attachment sent to authors, February 9, 2015.

45. Craig Nessan and Dwight DuBois, e-mail message to authors, February 9, 2015, which included the model resolution as an attachment.

46. Dwight DuBois, *Equipping Pastors Conversations* (Des Moines, IA: Center for Renewal, 2011), www.theologyofwork.org/uploads/general/Equipping_Pastors_Conversations_by_Dwight_DuBois.pdf, 1 (accessed February 8, 2015). These findings and many subsequent findings (including the surprising finding that pastors and laypeople hold diametrically opposing views on this topic) will be the backbone of his forthcoming book, working title: *The Scattering: Releasing God's People for Ministry in Daily Life*, to be published by Wipf and Stock Publishers, 2016.

47. DuBois, *Equipping Pastors Conversations*, 1.

48. Ibid., 4, 6, 13.

49. Ibid.

50. Ibid.

51. Ibid.

52. Ibid., 15.

53. Ibid., 18, quoting Darrell L. Guder, *The Continuing Conversion of the Church* (Grand Rapids: Eerdmans, 2000), 178–79.

54. DuBois, *Equipping Pastors Conversations*, 16, citing Elton True-blood, *The Company of the Committed* (San Francisco: Harper and Row, 1961) as quoted in *The Equipping Pastor*, 2.

55. DuBois, *Equipping Pastors Conversations*, 14.

56. Nessan, *Neighborliness*, 1.

57. Ibid.

58. Ibid., 2–3.

59. Judith McWilliams Dickhart, *Church-Going Insider or Gospel-Carrying Outsider: A Different View of Congregations* (Chicago, IL: Division for Ministry, Evangelical Lutheran Church in America, 2002), 83.

60. Ibid., 92.

61. Bob Victorin-Vangerud, e-mail message to authors, December 12, 2014.

62. Graber Miller, "Transforming Vocation," 29–48.

63. Ibid., 32–33, quoting Menno Simons, "True Christian Faith," in *The Complete Writings of Menno Simons, c. 1496–1561,* ed. J. C. Wenger, trans. Leonard Verduin (Scottdale, PA: Herald Press, 1956), 369.

64. Graber Miller, "Transforming Vocation," 35–36.

65. Ibid., 37.

66. Ibid., 42–43.

67. Ibid., 43, citing Ervin R. Stutzman, "Preacher's Calling: For John Ruth, It Meant a Lot," in *The Measure of My Days,* ed. Reuben Z. Miller and Joseph S. Miller (Telford, PA: Cascadia Publishing House, 2004), 147.

68. Graber Miller, "Transforming Vocation," 43.

69. Ibid., 44.

70. Ibid., 47–48.

71. Ryan Ahlgrim, e-mail message to authors, October 30, 2014.

72. Ryan Ahlgrim, e-mail message to authors, January 12, 2015.

73. John D. Roth, *Practices: Mennonite Worship and Witness* (Scottdale, PA: Herald Press, 2009), 96, 104.

74. Ibid., 147.

75. Ibid., 164.

76. Ibid., 211.

77. Patricia Rohrer, RN, MSN, First Mennonite Church, Richmond, Virginia, e-mail message to authors, January 26, 2015.

78. Father Roger Landry, "Pope Francis and the Reform of the Laity," *National Catholic Register,* April 11, 2013, www.ncregister.com/daily-news/pope-francis-and-the-reform-of-the-laity (accessed February 14, 2015).

79. Landry, "Pope Francis and the Reform of the Laity."

80. Landry, "Pope Francis and the Reform of the Laity."

81. *Evangelii Gaudium,* by Pope Francis, http://w2.vatican.va/content/francesco/en/apost_exhortations/documents/papa-francesco_esortazione-ap_20131124_evangelii-gaudium.html (accessed June 19, 2015).

82. Rebecca Ryskind Teti, "The Solution to Clericalism Is Not Simply to Have More Laity Involved inside the Church Walls," www.catholicvote.org/solution-to-clericalism-not-simply-more-laity/ (accessed January 19, 2015).

83. Anthony Shonis, "Ministry in an Age of Cubicle and Office Parks," *America: The National Catholic Review* http://americamagazine.org/issue/706/100/spirit-work (accessed December 15, 2014).

84. Gregory F. Augustine Pierce, *The Mass Is Never Ended: Rediscovering Our Mission to Transform the World* (Notre Dame, IN: Ave Maria Press, 2007), 42

85. Ibid., 9, 11.

86. Ibid., 111.

87. Paul Sparks, Tim Soerens, and Dwight J. Friesen, *The New Parish: How Neighborhood Churches Are Transforming Mission, Discipleship and Community* (Downers Grove, IL: InterVarsity Press, 2014), 8 (Nook edition).

88. The New Parish website, www.newparish.org/feature/conferences/ (accessed February 24, 2015).

89. Inhabit Conference website, http://inhabitconference.com/ (accessed February 24, 2015).

90. Loren Mead, *The Once and Future Church: Reinventing the Congregation for A New Mission Frontier* (Herndon, VA: The Alban Institute, 1991), 44

91. Sparks, Soerens, and Friesen, *New Parish,* 19 (Nook edition).

92. Ibid., 24 (Nook edition).

93. Ibid., 74 (Nook edition).

94. Ibid., 58 (Nook edition).

95. Ibid., 92 (Nook edition).

96. Ibid., 65 (Nook edition).

97. Ibid., 37 (Nook edition).

98. Ibid., 21 (Nook edition).

99. Cara Spaccarelli, response to research questionnaire e-mailed to authors, July 3, 2014.

100. David Robert Green, response to research questionnaire e-mailed to authors, July 9, 2014.

101. Lee Stephens, response to research questionnaire e-mailed to authors, July 7, 2014.

102. Scott Denman, response to research questionnaire e-mailed to authors, July 14, 2014.

103. Stephen Cuff, response to research questionnaire e-mailed to authors, July 27, 2014.

104. Stephanie Nagley, response to research questionnaire e-mailed to authors, July 21, 2014.

105. Sparks, Soerens, and Friesen, *New Parish,* 21 (Nook edition).

106. Member Mission Network website, http://www.membermission.org/about-member-mission/ (accessed February 25, 2015).

107. A. Wayne Schwab, *Where the Members Are the Missionaries: An Extraordinary Calling for Ordinary People* (Essex, NY: Member Mission Press, 2002) and *Living the Gospel: For Individuals and Small Groups* (Essex, NY: Member Mission Press, 2010).

108. www.stephenministries.org.

109. Mac Murray, response to research questionnaire e-mailed to authors, October 21, 2014.

110. Lee Anne Reat, response to research questionnaire e-mailed to authors, August 3, 2014.

111. Lee Anne Reat, response to research questionnaire e-mailed to authors, August 3, 2014.

112. Peyton G. Craighill, proposal e-mailed to authors, September 2, 2014.

113. Peyton G. Craighill, "Project DEO—Discipling Each Other in Christ," questionnaire e-mailed to authors, January 19, 2015.

114. Peyton G. Craighill, "Project DEO—Discipling Each Other in Christ," outline e-mailed to authors, November 16, 2014.

115. Davida Foy Crabtree, *The Empowering Church: How One Congregation Supports Lay People's Ministries in the World* (Herndon, VA: Alban Institute Publications, 1989), 10.

116. The Reverend Linda Barnes of Colchester Federated Church, Colchester, CT, telephone interview with the authors, March 24, 2015.

117. A Faith@Work article in the St. Paul's, Richmond, Virginia, monthly Epistle, October 2012.

118. www.thehighcalling.org.

119. Rick Warren, *A Purpose Driven Life* (Grand Rapids: Zondervan, 2002), 148.

120. Stephen R. Covey, *The 7 Habits of Highly Effective People: Powerful Lessons in Personal Change* (New York: Simon and Schuster, 2013), 247–72.

121. A Faith@Work article in the St. Paul's, Richmond, Virginia, monthly Epistle, February 2013.

122. A Faith@Work article in the St. Paul's, Richmond, Virginia, monthly Epistle, October 2012.

123. http://www.goodreads.com/quotes/104615-may-today-there-be-peace-within-may-you-trust-god (accessed June 20, 2015).

124. St. Paul's, Richmond, Virginia, monthly Epistle, September 2008.

125. John McClung, testimony e-mailed to the authors December 17, 2014.

126. www.huffingtonpost.com/kristi-york-wooten/one-year-later-how-painti_b_4418011.html (accessed March 11, 2015).

127. Testimony e-mailed to the authors, January 11, 2015.

128. A Faith@Work article in the St. Paul's, Richmond, Virginia, monthly Epistle, April 2010.

129. Op-ed, *Richmond Times Dispatch*, June 20, 2011.

130. Quoted in Dennis Ngien, *Giving Wings to the Soul* (Eugene, OR: Wipf & Stock, 2011), 1.

131. Sheryl A. Kujawa-Holbrook and Fredrica Harris Thompsett, *Born of Water, Born of Spirit: Supporting the Ministry of the Baptized in Small Congregations* (Herndon, VA: Alban Institute, 2010), 69.

132. Diana Butler Bass, *Christianity After Religion: The End of Church and the Birth of a New Spiritual Awakening* (New York: HarperCollins, 2012).

133. Bass, *Christianity After Religion,* 161, 170 (Nook edition).

134. Hadaway and Price data.

135. Dr. C. Kirk Hadaway, Office for Congregational Research, DFMS (Domestic and Foreign Missionary Society, The Episcopal Church), "Characteristics of Episcopal Churches by Size," (PowerPoint presentation, Standing Commission on Small Congregations, July 31, 2014).

136. www.ecbf.org.

137. Skye Jethani, "Advent Church: Is the Era of Mega-Ministries Ending?" *The High Calling*, December 15, 2014, www.thehighcalling.org/work/advent-church-era-mega-ministries-ending#.VKshLHtQ3EY (accessed January 5, 2015).

138. Barbara Brown Taylor, *The Preaching Life* (Lanham, MD: Rowman & Littlefield, 1993), 28.

139. Kerri Lenartowick, "Pope Francis Prays for Church to be 'Free of Clericalism,'" *National Catholic Register*, December 17, 2013, www.ncregister.com/daily-news/pope-francis-prays-for-church-to-be-free-of-clericalism#ixzz3PJGfYo00 (accessed January 18, 2015).

140. Loren Mead, "Lay Ministry Is at a Dead End," *LayNet* 15, no. 1 (Winter 2004): 7.

141. Mead, *Once and Future Church,* 35.

142. Bass, *Christianity After Religion*, 164 (Nook edition).

143. Presentation to Community of Hope class, at St. Mark's Episcopal Church, San Antonio, Texas, February 12, 2003.

144. We are indebted to the Reverend Robert J. Voyle and his essay, "Compassion and the Crazy Wisdom of Jesus or One Person's Way to Transform the World" (Hillsboro, OR: Clergy Leadership Institute, 2004), www.clergyleadership.com/appreciative-inquiry-resources/compassion.pdf.

145. Phyllis Tickle, *The Great Emergence: How Christianity Is Changing and Why* (San Francisco: Baker Books, 2012).

146. Thomas L. Friedman, *The World Is Flat: A Brief History of the Twenty-First Century* (New York: Farrar, Straus and Giroux, 2005).

147. Stephanie Spellers, *Radical Welcome: Embracing God, The Other, and the Spirit of Transformation* (New York: Church Publishing, 2006).

148. Ibid., 162.

149. Ibid., 162–63.

150. J. Fletcher Lowe Jr., *Baptism: The Event and the Adventure: A Collection of Resources for Baptism and Baptismal Living* (Leeds, MA: LeaderResources, 2005), 100–101.

151. Sue Mallory, *The Equipping Church* (Grand Rapids, MI: Zondervan, 2001), 58.

152. Dickhart, *Church-Going Insider*, 92.

153. R. Paul Stevens and Phil Collins, *The Equipping Pastor: A Systems Approach to Congregational Leadership* (Herndon, VA: Alban Institute, 1993), ix.

154. Ibid., 41.

155. Ibid.

156. Ibid., 127.

157. Ibid., 128–46.

158. Quoted by Dwight DuBois, *Equipping Pastors Conversations*, 13.

159. Taylor, *Preaching Life*, 28–32.

160. William E. Diehl, *The Monday Connection* (New York, NY: HarperCollins, 1991), 3.

161. William E. Diehl, *Thank God It's Monday!* (Minneapolis, MN: Fortress Press, 1982), 169.

162. Dwight Zscheile, *People of the Way: Renewing Episcopal Identity* (New York: Morehouse Publishing, 2012), 122.

163. Ibid., 117.

164. Stevens and Collins, *Equipping Pastor*, 127.

165. Pat Taylor Ellison and Patrick Keifert, *Dwelling in the Word: Deep Listening to God and One Another* (Robbinsdale, MN: Church Innovations, 2008), www.churchinnovations.org.

166. Peter Steinke, *How Your Church Family Works: Understanding Congregations as Emotional Systems* (Herndon, VA: Alban Institute, 1993, 2006).

167. Gilbert R. Rendle, *Leading Change in the Congregation: Spiritual and Organizational Tools for Leaders* (Herndon, VA: Alban Institute, 1998, 2007).

168. Jim Collins, *Good to Great: Why Some Companies Make the Leap and Others Don't* (New York, NY: HarperCollins Publishers, 2001) and *Good*

to *Great and the Social Sectors: A Monograph to Accompany Good to Great* (New York, NY: Harper Business, 2005).

169. Ron Heifetz, *The Practice of Adaptive Leadership: Tools and Tactics for Changing Your Organization and the World* (Boston, MA: Harvard Business Press, 2009).

170. Schwab, *Where the Members Are the Missionaries*, www.member-mission.org, and the workbook *Living the Gospel* by A. Wayne Schwab and Elizabeth S. Hall.

171. Diehl, *Monday Connection*, 3

172. Crabtree, *Empowering Church*, 1–2.

173. Corinne Ware, *St. Benedict on the Freeway: A Rule of Life for the 21st Century* (Nashville, TN: Abingdon Press, 2011).

174. Jack Fortin, telephone conversation with the authors, January 20, 2015.

175. Crabtree, *Empowering Church*, 3–4.

176. http://theworkshop-sa.org.

177. Pierce, *Mass Is Never Ended,* 115–18.

178. www.thehighcalling.org/work/earth-it-heaven-prayer-young-professionals#.VNZ7wi5Q3EZ (accessed February 1, 2015).

179. Jack Fortin, telephone conversation with the authors, January 20, 2015.

180. World Council of Churches, and Willem Adolph Visser 't Hooft, *The Evanston Report, The Second Assembly of the World Council of Churches, 1954* (New York: Harper and Brothers, 1955), 168.

181. Elton Trueblood, *Your Other Vocation* (New York: HarperCollins, 1952, 1976), 57–58.

182. Pierce, *Mass Is Never Ended,* 75.

183. Ibid., 116.

Selected Bibliography

Adams, David. *Power Lines: Celtic Prayers About Work.* Harrisburg, PA: Morehouse, 2000.

Bakke, Raymond, William Hendricks, and Brad Smith. *Joy at Work: Bible Study Companion.* Seattle: PVG, 2005.

Diehl, William H. *Ministry in Daily Life: A Practical Guide for Congregations.* Alban Institute Publication No. 174. Washington, DC: Alban Institute, 1996.

Fortin, Jack. *The Centered Life: Awakened, Called, Set Free, Nurtured.* Minneapolis: Augsburg Fortress, 2006.

Greene, Mark, *Supporting Christians at Work: A Practical Guide for Busy Clergy*. Chicago: Evangelical Lutheran Church in America, 2003.

Grenz, Linda L. and J. Fletcher Lowe, editors. *Ministry in Daily Life: A Guide to Living the Baptismal Covenant.* New York: Domestic and Foreign Missionary Society, 1996. http://arc.episcopalchurch.org/ministry/daily.htm (accessed April 20, 2015).

Hammond, Pete. "Ten Ways to Support Ministry in the Workplace" www.intheworkplace.com/apps/articles/default.asp?articleid=68288&columnid=1935 (accessed March 20, 2015)

Hammond, Pete, R. Paul Stevens, and Todd Svanoe. *The Marketplace Annotated Bibliography: A Christian Guide to Books on Work, Business and Vocation.* Downers Grove, IL: InterVarsity Press, 2002.

Hope, Susan. *Mission-Shaped Spirituality: The Transforming Power of Mission*. New York: Seabury Books, 2010.

Kraemer, Hendrik. *A Theology of the Laity.* Vancouver: Regent College Publishing, 2005.

Larive, Armand E. *After Sunday: A Theology of Work.* New York: Bloomsbury Academic, 2004.

Lowe, J. Fletcher, Jr. *Baptism: The Event and the Adventure: A Collection of Resources for Baptism and Baptismal Living.* Leeds, MA: LeaderResources, 2005.

Mead, Loren. *The Once and Future Church: Reinventing the Congregation for a New Mission Frontier.* Washington, DC: Alban Institute, 1991.

Neill, Stephen Charles and Hans-Ruedi Weber, editors, *The Layman in Christian History*, Philadelphia, PA: Westminster Press, 1963

O'Connor, Elizabeth. *Cry Pain, Cry Hope: Thresholds of Purpose.* Waco, TX: Word Books, 1987.

Pierce, Gregory. *The Mass Is Never Ended: Rediscovering Our Mission to Transform the World.* Notre Dame, IN: Ave Maria Press, 2007.

Rendell, Gilbert R. *Leading Change in the Congregation: Spiritual and Organizational Tools for Leaders.* Herndon, VA: The Alban Institute, 1998.

Rowthorn, Anne. *The Liberation of the Laity.* Eugene, OR: Wipf and Stock, 2000.

Sayers, Dorothy: Why Work? http://centerforfaithandwork.com/article/why-work-dorothy-sayers

Schwab, A. Wayne. *When the Members Are the Missionaries: An Extraordinary Calling for Ordinary People.* Essex, NY: Member Mission Press, 2002.

Schwab, A. Wayne and Elisabeth S. Hall. *Living the Gospel: A Workbook for Individuals and Small Groups.* Hinesburg, VT: Member Mission Press, 2010.

Spellers, Stephanie. *Radical Welcome: Embracing God, The Other, and the Spirit of Transformation.* New York: Church Publishing, 2006.

Stevens, R. Paul. *The Other Six Days: Vocation, Work, and Ministry in Biblical Perspective.* Grand Rapids: Wm. B. Eerdmans Publishing Co, 2000.

Theology of Work Project. "Equipping Churches Empower and Collaborate with People in the Congregation to Lead the Ministry" www.theologyofwork.org/key-topics/the-equipping-church/how-can-we-equip-our-people-for-gods-work-in-the-world/equipping-churches-empower-and-collaborate-with-people-in-the-congregation/ (accessed April 20, 2015).

Theology of Work Project. "How Can We Equip Our People for God's Work in the World?" www.theologyofwork.org/key-topics/the-equipping-church/how-can-we-equip-our-people-for-gods-work-in-the-world/ (accessed April 17, 2015).

Thompson, William David. *On the Job Prayers.* Chicago: ACTA Publications, 2006.

CPSIA information can be obtained
at www.ICGtesting.com
Printed in the USA
LVOW08s0602060717
540420LV00001B/21/P